HOME
ON THE RANGE

The Complete Practice Guide for the Golf Range

By Doug S. McDonald

Golf in the 80's, Seattle, Washington

HOME ON THE RANGE
The Complete Practice Guide
for the Golf Range

By Doug S. McDonald

Published by: Golf in the 80's
                   P.O. Box 16590-1
                   Seattle, WA 98116 USA

Illustrations: Randy Jones
Index: Carmen Miller
Cover Design: Christine Hess, T. Thomas, Doug McDonald
Back Cover Photo: Noreen Kilpatrick
Text, Photos, Design: Doug McDonald

Library of Congress Catalog Card Number: 96-94083
ISBN: 0-9628642-9-3 : $15.95 Softcover

Warning—Disclaimer
Consult with your physician before participating in golf or any sport. The purpose of this manual is to educate and entertain. The author and Golf in the 80's shall have neither liability nor responsibility to any person or entity with respect to any injury, loss, or damage caused, or alleged to be caused, directly or indirectly by the information contained in this book.

I've been blessed with a most amazing wife and the greatest parents.

To T.T., Greta and Mac.

Contents

ACKNOWLEDGMENT

This book was in no small way finished with the copy editing and creative suggestions of Dan Ito, Tom Marshall, Mark Granberg, and especially Steve Juetten.

For their help and support I am indebted to: Mike Yamashita, Carmen Miller, Tom Boozer, Morrie Kuhlman, Tracy Cleveland, Dan and C.J. Kosco, Bruce McCoy, John Webster, Tim Halm, Scott Milzer, Greg Hickman, David Abrams and Bobbette Jones, Patrick Marshall, Bob Scheld, The Varons—Mike, Pearl, and Al, Michael Nikinen, and Jim Brown.

A very special thanks to Joann Brislin.

To the incredibly photogenic models who appear throughout the book—Hollywood's been calling! On computers and software, a warm round of applause for Jeff Angus and Jack Oelshalger.

I would also like to give gratitude to my golfing buddies—the more I looked at their swings, the more I saw an urgent need for this book. To: Keith Kawaguchi, Eric Brolin, Glen Pastika, Colin Gants, Ramesh Motwani, Yong Lee, Hans Aarhus, Eric Berry, Vince Rankin, Dave Spurgeon—thanks boys!

And thank you, Dan Poynter: your book has been a great inspiration.

Thanks to:

The University of Washington Driving Range Crew:
Especially to Jim Seagren for his continued support. Also Rene, Dave, Marvin, Josh, Scott, Aidan, Niles, Brad, Pete, Karl, Brian, and Brian, Marty, Frank, Toshi, Fred, and all the rest.

The Jackson Park Golf Course Crew:
Mark Granberg, Ki-Tae Pak, Steve Wozeniak, Dan Jarvie, Jamie Sherman, Chris Francis, Dave Anderson, Noreen Kilpatrick, Bill Logsdon, Bob Johnson, Jack Kelly, Dick Rovig, Art Schreiber, Bruce Wilkins, Doug Coleman, Bob Rutzel, Otto Pfieffer, and Rudy Finne, et al.

The Redbird Sports Crew:
Jay and Anne Turner, Chris, P.T., Keith, Tracy, Dick, and Boss.

The CCS Crew:
Bennett, Greg, Karen, Joe, Ryan, and the rest.

And thanks especially to my students—you have taught me much.
I'm sure I've left out some very important people—but rest assured, you helped and I appreciate it.

INTRODUCTION

I took up golf in September of 1980 at the age of 25. I had never played before, and like many others before and after me, I was hooked. I wanted to know everything about the sport, and I wanted to learn it no later than the following day.

Back then, many books on the golf swing were written by the best players ever—Nicklaus, Palmer, Player, Snead, Hogan, etc.

Although in hindsight I now know that most of the instruction was sound, at the time, I found these books to have three major drawbacks:

1) Being told in precise detail what these great golfers felt happening inside *their* severely talented bodies had little to do with my game. Some of the instruction helped, but most missed the mark because I lacked their physical ability.

2) None of the books told me how to *identify and correct* a specific problem right then and there, while I was practicing at the range.

3) There was a dearth of information about *how* to practice. Needing the kind of direction that comes from having a specific routine laid out in front of me, I wasted a lot of time learning poor practice habits.

Well, you now have in your hands a golf book written by me. And rest assured, I am *not* one of the best golfers in the world. Not especially young, flexible, coordinated, or powerful—and I'll bet you and I are a lot alike.

For example:

I like to hear things put into simple terms, with visual images that are easy to relate to. And I need instruction presented in an orderly way with each step building on the previous one. Also, rather than a single method set in stone, I find it helpful to choose from different options, picking out what works best for me. After all, with a world full of so many different body types, and such varying degrees of ability, how can there be a single, universally applicable way to play golf?

In writing this book, my goal has been to provide you with coaching *as* you practice— a book to use at the driving range to fix a problem then, right in that moment. I want you to be able to look up your bad shots and *quickly* track down a cure—as you're hitting balls, not when you get back home. I've also included very detailed practice routines and methods to help make your range sessions as productive as possible.

USING THIS BOOK

Just like fixing the golf swing, there are many ways to take advantage of this book. You could start on page one and read all five chapters in order. Or after reading Chapter One, you might dive right into the most unique parts of the book—the Problems and Solutions sections (Chapters Three and Five). The bulleted items in these two chapters include various options to fix your specific problems. When you run into a snag in your game, look up the problem, scan the subheadings, then try the cures.

For example, suppose at the range you're hitting shots that start to the left of where you're aiming, before curving dramatically to the right. Take a break and open this book to Full Swing Problems and Solutions, which is Chapter Three on page 61. In the directory titled *In This Chapter*, you'll find Shots to the Right listed on page 63. Go to that page, and if you're not sure what your bad shot is called, use the diagrams in the margins to find the same shaped shot you're experiencing. In this case, it's the Pull Slice diagram on page 65 that depicts the shot you've been hitting. Scanning down the page you'll find these subheadings: Ball Position, Address, and Swing Path, with each followed by bulleted cures.

Try the most logical of these headings first—for example, if you've never spent time improving your swing path, maybe a possible cure resides under that heading.

Many of the bulleted cures include a page number referring to additional information in the Basic Instruction chapters. Study these references later, when you have the time at home. That way, you'll spend your range time hitting balls and less time reading.

It's important to remember that this book uses your *bad* shots to point you toward help. For example, if while working on Swing Plane you notice that the ball is going fairly straight but not very far, don't look for the answer under Swing Plane in the Full Swing Basics section. Look instead under No Power on page 93 of the Problems and Solutions section—lack of power, *not* Swing Plane, is the problem you are experiencing.

ABOUT HOME ON THE RANGE

Many of the ideas in *Home on the Range* are not mine originally. But they are presented in a way that is. All the instruction is simple, straightforward, and without gimmicks.

These cures work with every level of golfer, from the total beginner to the single digit handicapper, and all of the instruction can be used by women as well as men.

For you lefties out there: although written from a right handed perspective, everything here can be turned around—and that's probably the way you've been operating since finding out you were left handed.

Also, most of the Full Swing Problems and Solutions apply to iron shots, unless otherwise noted for woods.

I purposely used amateur models to depict the correct positions so you would be able to relate to them. The swings on TV may look slightly better, but my golfers are much easier to copy. And besides, they're still in the top 1% of all golfers on the planet!

And one last thing--you may notice that, because of the nature of the golf swing, some of the same cures are suggested for very different problems scattered throughout the book. I decided against repeating the same cures over and over throughout the book, and instead to use reference numbers to send you to the page where the original cure is spelled out. In this way I have cut down on the size of the book (saving paper and added expense for both of us) and kept the information more centrally located.

After 11 years of teaching over 8,500 students, I am convinced of one thing: Most of you have the ability to become very fine golfers—no matter your age, gender or ability in other sports. It depends on how much time you practice and how well you incorporate the ideas in this book into your practice routine.

CHAPTER ONE

AT HOME ON THE RANGE

You don't have to be young, strong, or talented to play better golf, and that opens the door for most of us. Everyone—from rank beginners happy just to get their ball airborne, to scratch golfers who need to be able to work the ball right-to-left—can use the range to improve.

WHAT can be done at the range? Although the *driving* in driving range encourages some to swing only their woods, you can work on every facet of the game: full swing, pitches, chips, putts, and a variety of strategic and getting-out-of-trouble shots. Take this book with you to the range: it will make your practice sessions as efficient and productive as possible.

WHEN should you go to the range? Some golfers visit the practice range only when their slightly curving shots graduate to full-fledged slices, or when the annual company golf day approaches. It's only natural to stop by the range when flaws in your swing start to increase your scores, or to prepare for a company tournament, but the driving range is a great place to visit routinely as well. Research shows that practice on a consistent basis yields the best results. Making practice sessions part of your routine helps keep the strengths of your game sharp and provides time to work on weaknesses away from the course.

When your schedule won't permit an 18-hole round of golf, a trip to the range can be a great substitute. Or when rain keeps you off the course, visit a covered range instead of waiting for the weather to clear up. You can sneak in an hour of practice time at lunch or after work. Working at the range during the winter months keeps your game from getting stale and relieves you from the "I'm starting all over again" feeling when spring finally comes. Two to three sessions a week is a reasonable goal.

WHERE can you find a range? There are different types of ranges. Many golf courses have ranges where you can practice or warm up before playing. Some ranges are not associated with courses; they are stand-alone practice and teaching facilities only. Check your phone book for location and hours.

WHY should you go to the range?
1. A REPEATING SWING Developing a swing you can count

on takes practice. Hitting balls at the range without the pressures of the golf course—the sand trap ahead and the approaching group behind—contributes to a dependable swing.

2. RELIABLE YARDAGE The ability to mentally gauge yardage and knowing the distance each club in your bag supplies is as important to you as to a professional. That's why most driving ranges put up yardage signs. Practicing toward these signs tells you how far an average shot travels with each of your clubs.

3. CONFIDENCE AND CONCENTRATION The range is a great place to improve your confidence and powers of concentration—two mental aspects closely tied to the physical components of the golf swing. Familiarity with the kind of shot you normally hit with each club improves your confidence before you swing. Your focus improves, too: you can concentrate on the shot at hand without the distractions of the golf course. Not only will your technique improve, you'll learn to train your attention on the ball and where you want it to go—the same thoughts you should have in mind out on the course.

4. MUSCLE MEMORY At the range, you have the luxury of stopping at a trouble spot anywhere in your swing, improving that position, then holding this new arrangement for five to sixty seconds of reinforcement. As you'll see in later chapters, muscle memory can produce dramatic results.

5. TAKING A LESSON Hitting range balls with your pro watching is one of the best ways to learn about your swing. He or she will suggest ways to straighten out the flight of your shots and increase their distance.

6. HITTING GOLF BALLS IS JUST PLAIN FUN!

The University of Washington Driving Range.

Safety Rules   Practice Safe Golf

1. Make sure no one is near you when swinging a club.

2. Don't get close to someone else when they are swinging a club.

3. Don't step in front of the tee line. Don't go onto the range to collect balls after your bucket runs out! If you accidentally let go of your club or lose a clubhead, don't just mosey on out onto the range to rustle it up. Talk to someone working there; they'll find a way to get it back to you.

4. Take a position where you won't hit or be hit by the person in the stall next to you. It's possible for the ball to come off the clubface at a right (or left) angle. Look at the person hitting in the stall to your left as you face out in the direction of the range; from their ball draw an imaginary line out toward your stall perpendicular to their line of flight. Stay behind that line. If you hear the ball whizzing past your left ear, it's time to move back.

5. On the chipping/pitching green, be aware of incoming shots when it's time to collect your balls. On the other side of the coin, watch out for people picking up their balls in your line of fire.

6. To avoid arguments at a busy range, find out the waiting policy for an empty stall. Do people take a number to wait their turn, or do they reserve a spot by placing a full bucket of balls next to a soon-to-be-vacated stall?

A DAY AT THE RANGE

Many golfers go to driving ranges with one thing in mind—hitting the ball enormous distances. However, inconsistent and inaccurate full swings, poor putting, or a second-rate short game may also be keeping you out of Fred Couples' foursome.

When spending the day at the range, you can work on *all* parts of the game, not just hitting the ball farther. Here are some suggestions to make your time more productive:

BEFORE YOU GO When going to your regular range, you already know what is available and the rules and policies that apply. If you are heading to a new range for the first time, call ahead to see about rental clubs if you need them, and check for any regulations that might affect your preparation. Most ranges have few guidelines beyond safety concerns, though the rules at some facilities might differ. I know of a range that won't allow golf bags taken in because some customers were pouring the range balls into their bags and stealing them! (Range balls are not made as well, and generally don't fly as far, as the balls sold in stores. These thieves did not do themselves any favors by taking them out on the course.)

Other range restrictions might include no golf shoes and no shag bags—those bags of old beat-up golf balls you've been saving.

DRESS FOR SUCCESS Wear clothes that allow comfort and freedom of movement in whatever weather conditions await you. In many parts of the country during the fall, winter, and spring, wearing layers of clothing is a sensible strategy. You can remove or add a layer if need be. Avoid bulky, thick shirts and sweaters—they restrict the swing. Also, watch out for noisy windbreakers and jackets: the rustling can be very distracting during the golf swing. You have a greater chance of staying warm by keeping your head covered; consider wearing a hat, earmuffs, or a hooded sweatshirt. Some ranges are even equipped with heaters blowing hot air into the stalls.

In the summer, make sure to carry a good sunscreen in your bag (SPF 15 or higher). Skin cancer is on the rise and golfers are in a high-risk group. Wear light-colored, loose-fitting clothing during the hotter months. A hat with a brim is helpful if your range doesn't have a roof.

Golf shoes are a matter of personal preference and range rules. Some golfers like to wear the same spiked golf shoes to the range that they wear out on the course. (Besides, they make that neat noise when you walk on the concrete.) Wearing golf shoes is a good idea when hitting off grass tees: gripping the ground with spikes provides extra leverage during the swing.

However, your spikes won't dig in when hitting off rubber mats, and you can find your feet substantially higher than the ball—tennis shoes might feel more comfortable on the mats. Wear appropriate shoes on the putting green—nothing with high heels or sharp soles. When wearing spiked golf shoes, be especially careful not to damage the putting surface by dragging your feet across the greens.

HAVE A PLAN Go to the range with a task in mind. Although it can sometimes be painful, review your last time out on the course and identify weak points in the two big areas of your game—full swing and short game. (See **Evaluating Your Game** below.) Choose *one* project in each area. In the full swing it might be correcting your slice with the 1-wood. On the short game side, maybe getting those fifteen-foot putts closer to the hole is a priority. Spend your session focused on just those goals.

EVALUATING YOUR GAME To decide which part of your game to work on at the range, review your most recent round of golf. What kept you from shooting the score you had hoped for? Poor drives? Mediocre irons? A lousy short game? Or a day on the greens that encourages you to buy a new putter?

An accurate picture of your strengths and weaknesses may be revealed by keeping track of pertinent statistics on your scorecard. First, make sure to get your own scorecard, even if someone else is keeping score for the group. At the bottom of the scorecard write down the word "putts" where you would normally write the name of a person in your foursome. After jotting down your score for each hole, put down the number of putts it took to get the ball into the cup. Check the scorecard at the end of the round for your putting total, and for clues about the rest of your short game. For example, when averaging more than two putts per hole, it suggests not only that your putting needs work, but also that your chips and pitches aren't getting close enough to one-putt.

Use the scorecard to record any other information that helps focus your next practice session. Did you take more than one shot coming out of a sand trap? Jot it down. Where do you tend to hit your tee shots? Are you consistently to the left, consistently to the right, or consistently inconsistent? Make a note if your approach shots are always falling short of, or airmailing, the greens. If weather conditions confused you, write that down. Scribble questions on the back of your card and run them past your golf instructor at your next lesson.

TIME TO WARM UP Do some easy stretching to warm up the muscles—arms, legs, shoulders, trunk, and back—used when swinging the club. Jack Nicklaus has said he is hitting the

Figure 2
A and B

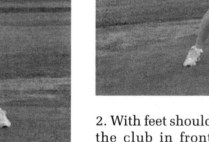

Figure 1

ball as well, or better, than he did when he was younger, just by stretching every day.

Here are four good stretches to get you going:
1. With your feet shoulder-width apart and knees flexed, bend from the waist to touch your toes. It doesn't matter if you actually do touch your toes, the goal is to loosen up your back. Don't bounce up and down or force yourself to go lower. Just hang there; try to relax into this stretch, and hold it for at least thirty seconds. **(Figure 1)**

2. With feet shoulder-width apart, hold the club in front of you with your thumbs pointing toward each other, one hand down by the clubhead and the other at the grip end. Slowly swing back and forth, as if taking a golf swing. Make sure your shoulders turn—don't just lift your arms. Keep it slow and relaxed, and aim for a full range of motion. **(Figure 2)** Make this motion similar to a good golf swing and you'll improve your shots while warming up your muscles and joints.
3. This time put the club behind your back, hooked with your elbows. As in the exercise above, slowly swing back and forth. Try to point the left end of the club behind the ball during the backswing, and get the other end past the ball in the follow-through. Move slowly and stay relaxed. **(Figure 3)**

Figure 3
A and B

4. Take slow-motion practice swings holding two or three clubs together.

A complete review of golf exercises is beyond the scope of this book, but I can recommend a fine text on that subject. It's called *Exercise Guide to Better Golf*, by Jobe, Yocum, Mottram, and Pink. The authors have included an entire chapter on stretches, and another on strengthening exercises. All the exercises are for golf-specific muscles—those used during the swing.

WHERE TO START Once you are at the range and have paid for a bucket of balls, your practice strategy comes into effect. Head for the putting green, not the driving areas. Starting with your short game is the most efficient and cost-effective use of your time and your range balls. You can work on your short

game for hours with a single bucket of balls and, when you shift to the full swing, still have your whole bucket left to hit out onto the range.

Also, when you progress from putting to chipping, pitching, bunker shots, and then to the full swing, you are moving from less to more complex movements; putting and chipping involve the fewest moving parts.

Still not convinced that you should begin your practice session with the short game? Consider this: starting out with the full swing taxes your big muscles. By the time you get to the practice greens, the sense of touch that is so important to the short shots is gone. You'll end up hitting the little chips with the same feel you had while trying to crush the ball with the driver; your control over the distance for the short shots will be lost.

GET TO WORK! Pull out your putter and a couple of balls and find a spot on the putting green. Try some short putts to build your confidence, gradually moving farther away from the hole.

Practice all the different putts awaiting you during a round of golf—long, short, uphill, downhill, side hill, on the fringe, etc.

Make sure to rehearse the same good habits you take onto the golf course. If necessary, clean your ball and putter blade before each stroke. Spend time reading the putt. Go through your putting routine, including a practice stroke. When working on a specific problem, take your practice strokes with the remedy in mind. For example, with most of your putts racing past the cup, pull this book out of your bag, look up **Short Game Problems, Putting, Too Far**, and run through the checklist of solutions. There you will see that one possible answer is to take the club back a shorter distance. If that seems to apply to your stroke, take your practice swings emphasizing a shorter backswing.

Move to the chipping and pitching green. Because putting and chipping are very similar, and because you

just finished your putting practice, try some chip shots first.

Take ten balls out of your basket to chip with. Hit balls from one position, then pick them up and move to a new spot. Vary the distance and complexity of the shot. Work with ten balls for the following reasons: it's easy to calculate your percentage of good shots when working with an even ten: if one of your goals is to chip seventy percent of your shots within five feet of the hole, and you land seven balls in that five-foot zone, Eureka! Working with a set number of balls also pays off when retrieving them—you know how many balls to collect even when they get mixed up with other peoples' shots. And your path to the hole won't get so jammed up with balls that they hit one another, keeping you from seeing the true outcome of your shot. Finally, when you have to stop after ten shots to gather up your balls, you have the opportunity to refresh your concentration and choose a new chip or pitch to try.

After chipping, hit some pitches and bunker shots—at least thirty shots of each.

Practice pitching for many reasons: (1) Pitching is a miniature full swing. In other words, your full swing improves along with this shorter shot; (2) Practice pitching to raise your confidence level—you soon won't dread facing this shot out on the golf course, and the resulting aggressiveness will

> **Starting with your short game is the most efficient and cost-effective use of your time and your range balls.**

do wonders for your score; and, (3) pitching is a great way to warm up for full shots with your irons and woods.

Ready. . . It's time to hit some full shots. Survey the scene at the practice tees. Sometimes the crowd dictates where you can hit, but when possible, choose a spot or stall where there are yardage markers to aim at. Use these to gauge the distance of your shots. (Remember, range balls have been hit so many times they usually don't fly as far as brand new store-bought balls. And in wet, cold conditions they travel even shorter distances.)

When hitting off grass tees try to find a level spot that's not barren, unless you want to work on uneven lies off hardpan. If you're at a multi-tiered range with two floors of stalls to hit from, keep in mind that shots travel farther from the upper-story stalls. Because the ball starts from a higher point, it moves farther out as it drops to the ground.

Aim. . . Before hitting any balls, pick a target or find some reference point to aim at—for example, a yardage sign, flag, tree, or telephone pole. Set your body parallel to the target line (the imaginary line stretching from your ball to that target). For an alignment aid when hitting from grass tees, put a club on the ground just to the outside of the ball; make sure it is parallel to the target line and placed

Figure 4:
Parallel clubs used as alignment aids.

Figure 5: Edges of mat are parallel to target line.

far enough from the ball to avoid being hit. Lay down a second club for your feet and body. **(Figure 4)**

Depending on the part of the country you live in, you might have to hit from a rubber mat instead of grass. If that's the case, you have an advantage: the straight edges of the mat make a handy alignment aid. Stand behind your mat and turn it so an imaginary line through the spot on the mat where the ball will be points to your target—this is your target line. This line should be parallel to the outside edges of the mat. **(Figure 5)** Position the ball on this target line (unless that part of the mat is excessively worn down), and align your clubface and body to the straight edges of the mat. **(See Aiming and Alignment, page 27.)** Now you are aiming in the same direction as the mat.

Fire! Okay, you're ready to hit that first ball. By this time you will have decided on your project for the day. For this discussion, let's say the current problem is slicing the ball to the right. You've looked up **Full Swing Problems, Shots to the Right** in this book, and after reviewing the checklist, you decide to work on your blocking problem. Pick a bulleted cure—for example, touching your forearms after impact—and think of this one correction while taking two practice swings without the ball. Then hit a ball and, regardless of where it goes, ask yourself if your arms touched. Take two more practice swings without the ball, concentrating on your arms, and then hit another ball. Follow this routine for each shot. Ignore the bad shots, which are a natural consequence of trying to learn a new habit, and concentrate solely on refining the movements of your body.

Practice swings make your range sessions more fruitful. Many good (smart) golfers take a minimum of one or two practice swings for every ball they hit. Try some of these swings in slow motion; this makes it easier to isolate a problem in your swing and to focus on the correction. Practice swings also give your muscles time to recover before the next swing with the ball.

Make each shot count—don't fall into the trap of racing through the bucket of balls. Without pausing between shots, your swing will deteriorate, and faulty mechanics can quickly become permanent. For a productive session at the range, figure on at least thirty seconds per ball—a small bucket of 45 balls should take roughly one-half to three-quarters of an hour to finish. To help slow down, try this tip from Lee Trevino and Tom Watson: Put the bucket a couple of feet away from where you are swinging and keep all of the balls in it. The process of taking one ball out at a time and setting it on the grass or mat gives you the chance to go through your pre-shot routine. Executing your pre-shot routine **(see Full Swing Basics, Odds and Ends, Pre-shot Routine, page 57)** before every swing helps keep you under control at the range, just as it does on the course. With all of the balls dumped out into a pile, it's easy to shift into auto-pilot—reaching for another ball to hit without much thought about what happened in the previous swing, or what you will be trying to do with the next swing. It's like eating potato chips.

Take rest breaks to avoid the lapses in concentration that come with fatigue. Studies have shown that compared to practicing a long time without taking a break, practicing in smaller chunks of time, with many breaks, speeds up the learning process. Try to hit balls for about twenty to thirty minutes and then take a rest. You can still be productive while resting: look around the other hitting stalls and find a golfer with good balance and a smooth tempo. Take mental notes. Just by watching, you can start to incorporate these same fundamentals into your swing.

WARNING!!

Take all unsolicited advice at the range with a grain of salt. Many people are only too happy to share their secrets for the perfect golf swing. Unless they have the kind of swing seen on TV—balanced, good tempo, powerful yet seemingly effortless—ignore their advice. Smile politely and go back to work on your project for the day.

AT THE RANGE: BEFORE YOUR ROUND

How many times have you looked at your scorecard and winced at the scores on the first couple of holes, then dismissed those high numbers as "warm-up holes"? You can avoid the stiffness, nervousness, and big scores all too common to the first holes by using the range to warm up before your round. You'll feel as though you've already played a few holes before getting to that intimidating first tee.

To warm up productively before a round of golf, follow a similar but scaled-down version of your full-blown practice sessions at the range:

❖ Get to the golf course forty-five minutes to an hour before your tee time. Buy a small bucket—you only need to hit between 25 and 50 balls.

❖ Stretch and get loose before taking any swings, even practice swings. **(See A Day at the Range, Time to Warm Up, page 5.)** This helps you relax and avoid injury.

❖ Check out the greens first: spend ten minutes putting to get a feel for how fast the greens are and to help groove your putting stroke for the day. Hit some chips and pitches for the same reasons.

❖ Keep your pre-round thoughts simple. Think big thoughts—like shifting your weight, staying relaxed, or making solid contact with the ball. Reserve detailed thoughts about your right elbow and your left hip for a day at the practice range. Remember, your goal is to warm up, not overhaul.

❖ Next, find a spot to hit out into the range.

❖ Without the ball, take some easy practice swings using a sand wedge, pitching wedge, or a 9-iron. The added weight of the sand wedge makes it an ideal club to loosen up with. Try some half- or three-quarter swings when you start hitting shots; within the first five to ten balls, move up to full swing 9-irons. Stay with a full swing as you work your way through the longer clubs in your bag, hitting every other club—for example, all the odd numbered clubs. Hit a few shots with each club, through the woods. After five to ten swings with the woods (don't wear yourself out), finish the bucket of balls the same way you started: with some half-swing wedges. Finishing with wedge shots should help remind you to keep the same swing with your long and short clubs, and leave you with a good feel for the short shots out on the course.

❖ As you work through the bag, evaluate the conditions of the day. Are the fairways dry or wet? How much roll will you get? On a windy day, how much will your ball be blown around? Are you hitting your clubs their average distance, or is the wind sending your shots ten yards farther than normal? Cold weather affects your shots— because the ball won't compress as much at impact, it travels shorter distances. For all of the above, adjust accordingly on the course.

❖ Evaluate your shots and form a strategy. For example, with most of your shots going right, plan to aim down the left side of the fairway and let the ball curve back to the middle. In other words, play the swing you arrived at the course with—don't try to fix it in the few minutes before the round starts.

❖ Leave the range feeling loose and ready to play. Remember, your pre-round warm-up is not a practice session—don't make the mistake of hitting too many balls and leaving your game on the tee line. Save your concentration and energy for the day's round.

THE ONCE A YEAR TOURNAMENT: AVOID LOOKING LIKE A COMPLETE IDIOT

This section is for those of you who might have little time to devote to golf, yet every year you find yourself entered in a company tournament. Here is a concentrated schedule to get the most out of your limited time at the range.

General

❖ If you don't own golf clubs, consider borrowing some from a friend.

❖ Go to the range a minimum of three times a week for the two weeks before the tournament. Stay at least one hour during each session.

❖ Spend sixty percent of your practice time on your short game (putting, chipping, and pitching).

❖ During the other forty percent of your time, practice your full swing. Figure out which clubs you are hitting well, and spend at least half of this time practicing with your *weakest* clubs.

❖ Work on your full swing at home at least five minutes a day, swinging over a piece of carpet or welcome mat in your backyard or on your deck. *Don't* swing at anything on the mat— whiffle balls, cigarette butts, or anything else— but try to hit the same spot, over and over. Make sure the club touches the mat left of where the ball would be in your stance. **(See Divots, page 56.)** Focus on your balance and staying relaxed.

Full Swing

❖ Work on no more than two swing keys each session. Hit three shots in a row working with one swing thought, then three with the second. Repeat that pattern over and over—don't throw in any other things to work on.

❖ Stay relaxed with your upper body (shoulders, forearms, hands), no matter what you are working on.

❖ Always aim to hit your ball at a specific target— yardage signs, the flag sticks, or towards something on the horizon.

❖ Record your average distances with each club in your bag. Memorize these distances or write them down and keep them in your bag to refer to out on the course.

❖ Take two practice swings after each shot. It is better to hit thirty thoughtful shots than to race through three large buckets of balls.

❖ Concentrate on the basics—grip, address, weight shift, follow-through, etc. Don't do anything exotic, no matter what the person next to you suggests.

❖ Avoid advice from friends or fellow rangers, unless they routinely shoot below 80. (For eighteen holes, not nine.)

❖ Play by the rules. Buy the *USGA Rules of Golf* booklet at your local range or golf course. Study them— at times you'll be able to use the rules to your advantage.

❖ Learn proper etiquette, also discussed in the *Rules of Golf*. Everyone else on the course will appreciate it when you play quickly and efficiently. You will have a more pleasant round if the other groups behind your tournament are not screaming on every hole for you to hurry up. Here are five ways to pick up the pace:

1. Walk to your ball quickly.

2. Be prepared to hit as soon as it's your turn. If you're the person farthest from the hole, it's your turn.

3. Take only one practice swing before each shot.

4. Before putting, leave your golf bag between the green and the next tee box. When your group finishes putting, pick up your bag on the way to the next hole.

5. Whenever your ball heads toward trouble pick a landmark on the horizon to mark the spot where it might be. Walk directly toward that spot to find your ball. (The rules allow a maximum of five minutes to look for a lost ball.)

❖ Tee off with the longest club that you have confidence in; don't feel obligated to use a driver on every tee shot. It's better to hit a shorter shot down the middle than to hit the ball a long distance— into somebody's backyard.

Don't expect perfection— manage your temper and have fun.

❖ Play a couple of rounds in the weeks before your tournament, especially on *short* and *executive* courses. These are shorter courses designed specifically for novice golfers: most of the holes are short, and filled with people in the same boat as you—beginners. Like anything else, the more you participate the better you get.

❖ Be prepared with equipment— balls, tees, ball marker, towel, sunscreen, golf glove, rain gear, cloth tape, band aids, visor, greens repair tool, pencil and scorecard.

TAKING A LESSON

Whether you are a beginner who's decided to take up golf or an experienced player trying to sharpen your game, the range is a good place to seek professional help with a lesson.

Lessons come in two basic varieties—group and private. Group lessons provide an introduction to the game and usually cover the basics of the full swing, short game, putting, rules, equipment, and etiquette. They are a great starting point for beginners, or for better golfers coming back to the game after a long layoff. Group lessons have other advantages, too: (1) they are less expensive, which may be a real consideration if you are just giving the game a try; (2) they provide a relaxed setting to learn in; (3) you have the opportunity to hit (and mis-hit) lots of balls as your instructor works with each of your classmates; (4) you won't be the only one hitting shots that roll along the ground (worm-burners), or go straight left, straight up, or not at all; (5) a series of group lessons keeps you coming to the range on a regular schedule; and, (6) group lessons give you the opportunity to meet other golfers at the same level of the game—trade phone numbers and you'll have fellow golfers to play or practice with.

Private lessons, on the other hand, are ideal for golfers who benefit from a one-on-one setting, or for golfers in need of concentrated individual help diagnosing and curing swing flaws. They are usually more expensive than group lessons, but private sessions give you and your teacher the opportunity to work on *your* specific problems, without competition for the instructor's attention from ten other students. They also allow you to try subtle changes to find just the right correction. Another great option is a *videotaped* private lesson. Capturing the lesson on tape gives you a permanent record of everything said, and the ability to study your swing whenever you like. You will be able to try different moves on camera to get your body into the correct positions, to see if you really are changing your swing as much as it feels.

Whether you choose group or private lessons (or a combination), there is a very important decision to make—picking a teacher. Spend a few minutes, either on the phone or in person, going over the background, experience, teaching philosophy, etc., of various instructors. Look for good "chemistry" between the two of you. Does the pro say things in a way you understand clearly? Maybe this instructor comes highly recommended from a friend, but the same words your friend understands so clearly might not make any sense to you. What kind of learner are you? Do you need to *hear* detailed explanations, *feel* the correct position, *see* the skill demonstrated a number of times, or a combination of these? Do you like a no-nonsense approach to a lesson or do you enjoy the chance to talk about your various golfing experiences? Hook up with a teacher who meets your needs as a student. Ask around for recommendations, or watch different instructors in action as they give lessons. Keep your eyes open for a solid swing when playing with other people out on the golf course. Don't be shy—ask them where they learned to play. Many people have called me for lessons after playing golf with one of my students.

Once you choose your teacher, *you* must meet some responsibilities as a student.

First: Listen To Your Instructor. This may be more difficult than it sounds—he or she may ask you to try some techniques that feel terrible. *Trust your pro.* Remember, not only are you trying to learn new habits, but unless you are a total beginner, you will be trying to break old, bad habits at the same time. And you are bound to hit many strange-looking shots in the process of making the adjustments that lead to more consistent shots. Work only on the changes from your lesson; don't get sidetracked by a magazine article or a friend's advice. Also, it's not a bad idea to take notes during or immediately after the lesson to help your recollection later.

Second: Practice. You need to be willing to spend time at the range hitting balls to make a long-term change in your swing. Better players figure on hitting at least a thousand shots before they learn a new habit, and they are mentally prepared for the first five hundred to be less than successful.

Third: Communicate With Your Teacher. Bring specific questions to the lesson. Write them down when they come to you while practicing at the range or playing out on the course. When you have a *quick* question, snag your teacher at the range after he or she finishes with lessons for the day. Most will be willing to give you two or three minutes of their time (if not, it might be time to look for a new teacher). Make sure your question has to do with something you have already talked about in a previous lesson, and keep it short—don't try for a free full-blown lesson.

Follow up with regularly scheduled lessons. Don't schedule your next session until you've had time to become comfortable with the correct moves from the previous lesson.

TRUST YOUR PRO.
Remember, not only are you trying to learn new habits, but unless you are a total beginner, you will be trying to break old, bad habits at the same time.

Ten Commandments for the Range

1. WARM UP

2. GO TO THE RANGE WITH A GOAL IN MIND

3. GIVE YOURSELF ENOUGH TIME TO ACCOMPLISH YOUR GOAL

4. PUT PRESSURE ON YOURSELF—STAY UNTIL YOU HAVE ACCOMPLISHED YOUR GOAL, E.G., HIT SEVEN OF TEN CHIPS WITHIN FIVE FEET

5. PRACTICE YOUR SHORT GAME BEFORE WORKING ON YOUR FULL SWING

6. WORK ON A WEAKNESS IN YOUR GAME

7. AIM AT SOMETHING

8. NEVER WORK ON MORE THAN TWO SWING THOUGHTS AT A TIME

9. SIMULATE COURSE CONDITIONS—PRACTICE VISUALIZATION, PRE-SHOT ROUTINE, ETC.

10. STUDY AND MEMORIZE THE DISTANCES YOU HIT EACH OF YOUR CLUBS*

* Because of their inferior construction and constant use, range balls can travel one half to a full club shorter than regular golf balls.

CHAPTER TWO

FULL SWING BASICS

Would you like to hit the ball higher, straighter, farther? Are you looking for a fool-proof follow-through? Do you need to better understand Blocking, Casting, and Divots? Please read on. . .

GRIP

Many of the problems at impact, or even later in the golf swing, actually have their roots in a faulty grip. Your hands need to work together as a single unit during the swing. These three important characteristics of a correct grip allow your hands to work properly: (1) both palms facing each other, (2) the club resting in your fingers, not in your palms, and (3) both hands close together with no gaps between your fingers and the club.

Start by placing the grip of the club across the callus pad at the bottom of your left index finger, and extend it across your palm, so it hooks between the fleshy heel at the bottom of your left hand and the pad at the base of your index finger. The club should feel wedged between these two areas of your hand. **(Figure 6)** Close your fingers around the club; it now rests in the fingers of your left hand, not in the palm.

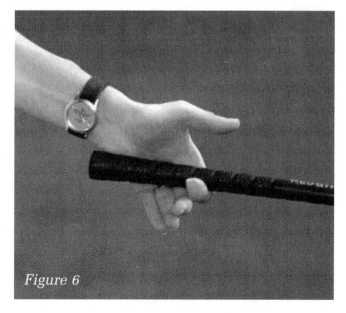

Figure 6

With the club in your fingers, a lot of the bottom of your left palm should be visible above the club's grip. Place your left thumb just to the right side of the shaft.

Now, connect your right hand to your left. Lay the club across the row of callus pads at the base of the fingers of your right hand, again making sure the grip rests mainly in your fingers, not in your palm. **(Figure 7, next page)** Holding the club in your palms inhibits the free hinging and un-hinging of your wrists, limiting power and consistency. Close the fingers of your right hand around the club, leaving a small gap between the index and middle finger. Fit the lifeline of your right palm over your left thumb to seamlessly connect your hands, like pieces of a jigsaw puzzle. Completely cover your left thumb with your right palm and thumb

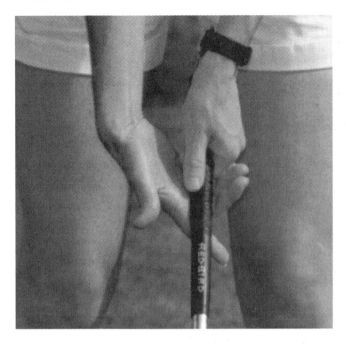

Figure 7:
Club placed in fingers of right hand.

pad, and rest your right thumb just to the left side of the shaft. You shouldn't be able to see much of your left thumb after your right hand gets on the club. Make sure your entire right hand, except the little finger, is on the club—watch especially your ring finger.

At this point decide whether to use an interlocking or an overlapping grip. Don't think of this as a permanent decision—it's a good idea to eventually try both. An overlapping grip, used by many of the best golfers in the world, places the right little finger in the groove between the left index and middle fingers. **(Figure 8A)** An interlocking grip intertwines the right little finger and left index finger. **(Figure 8B)** Choose the grip that is most comfortable.

Double check everything: make sure your palms are facing each other, both hands are close together with no gaps between your fingers and the club, and the club is resting in your fingers, not palms.

Figure 8A:
Overlapping grip.

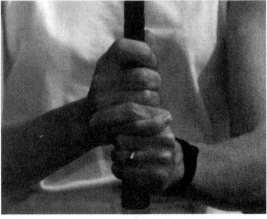

Figure 8B:
Interlocking grip.

Grip Pressure

Here's one of the biggest secrets in golf: most of the best golfers in the world swing with extremely *light* grip pressure. There isn't a conspiracy to keep this quiet, it's just that it's usually not emphasized. You have to read the golf magazines carefully and listen closely when the pros are interviewed to hear this—it's a common thread on the professional tours.

Light grip pressure does some important things for your swing: (1) it allows your wrists to hinge and unhinge freely, creating clubhead speed; (2) it helps to keep your forearms, shoulders and upper body relaxed, so they won't be tempted to race the club down to the ball—your legs get a chance to work instead; (3) you'll have more energy on the last three holes—it won't be like you've been chopping wood on the previous fifteen; and (4) you will probably hit more shots on the sweet spot, because of improved balance from a smoother, more controlled swing.

A tight grip on the club contributes to a swing dominated by your upper body. While this distorts swing path and clubface alignment, you'll also lose clubhead speed, balance, and may even hurt your back. In other words, you will probably hit short shots to the right, and be in need of traction.

Following are images used to achieve the correct grip pressure:

❖ Nancy Lopez and Joey Sindelar think about gripping an opened tube of toothpaste. They don't want *any* toothpaste oozing out during their swings—from beginning to end. To get a feel for this, try swinging a real uncapped, full tube of toothpaste.

❖ Paul Azinger imagines he's holding a stick of room-temperature butter: his goal is to keep the sides flat and the edges square throughout his swing. He doesn't want to push in the edges of the wrapper anywhere along the grip.

❖ Sam Snead tries to hold his club as lightly as he would a live bird, with enough pressure to keep the bird from flying away, but relaxed enough to avoid hurting it. Don't hold the club so loosely that your hands open up, even the tiniest bit, anywhere in your swing. Watch for this, especially at the top of your backswing and at the end of the follow-through.

The pros use these mental images for two reasons: (1) swinging with relaxed hands is key to their successful swings; that's why they come up with their own personalized way to grip the club, and (2) they constantly have to work on this—light grip pressure is not a habit, even after years of practice.

Whichever image clicks, both hands should have *equal* pressure on

> . . . the best golfers in the world swing with extremely *light* grip pressure.

the club, and your grip must be no tighter at the end of the swing than it was at address. That last part is probably the most difficult—*finish your swing with exactly the same light grip pressure you started with.*

It's impossible to keep a light pressure when your club's grips are old and slippery. Have new grips installed at least once a year—twice a year if you use your clubs more than a couple of times a week. One more thing: many amateur golfers believe the pros wear gloves on their left hands to be able to increase their grip pressure without the worry of getting blisters. In fact, they wear golf gloves for exactly the opposite reason: the leather of the golf glove grabs onto the brand new rubber of the grips, allowing them to relax their hands *even more* without the worry of the club coming loose during the swing.

◆   ◆   ◆   ◆   ◆

Figure 9:
Vertical alignment
of hands at impact.

Strong, Weak, Neutral

Note: much instruction has been written about the "V's" of the grip—the crease formed where the thumb and index fingers meet—and where they point when the hands are on the club. Because I've seen so many differently shaped hands with the "V's" pointing in every direction, I don't find this to be a reliable reference point. On the other hand, everyone can relate to the flat part of the back of the left hand, and the palm of the right, and those are the areas I prefer to base grip alignment on.

The position of your hands on the club has everything to do with where the ball goes—they have a direct affect on where the clubface points at impact. Because of the way we are built and the way our arms work, when relaxed and swinging well, our hands return to a vertical alignment at impact. That is, the back of the left hand and the palm of the right face the target as the ball is struck. **(Figure 9, previous page)**

By taking this hand alignment at impact into account we can now see how three basic grips affect ball flight:

Strong—Turning your hands slightly to the right, clockwise on the club, with the back of your left hand and the palm of your right pointing above and to the right of the target, should produce a *draw*—the ball curving gently right to left. With a good swing causing your hands to return to a neutral position at impact, the club's face points to the left. **(Figure 10, next page)** Many touring pros use a slightly strong grip because a right-to-left shot tends to travel farther than a left-to-right. However, the ball can *hook* (curving uncontrollably right to left) with a grip that is too strong.

Neutral—This grip is also seen on the professional tours. It starts at address with the back of the left hand and the right palm facing the target. **(Figure 11)** Take a good swing with this grip and the club should square up at impact, producing a straighter shot.

Weak—A left-to-right shot can result when starting with your hands turned counterclockwise on the club. With the back of your left hand and the palm of your right facing down to the ground between your ball and the target, the clubface opens as your hands return to their neutral alignment at impact, sending the ball to the right. **(Figure 12)** Although not many professionals use a weak grip, Jose Marie Olazabal is a notable exception.

Surprisingly, few pros count on hitting a straight shot. Everything—including clubface alignment, clubhead path, and the angle that the clubhead approaches the ball—has to be perfect at impact to keep the ball from curving. On the contrary, good golfers place their hands on the club carefully to complement their natural tendency to curve the ball slightly left (a draw), or to the right (a fade).

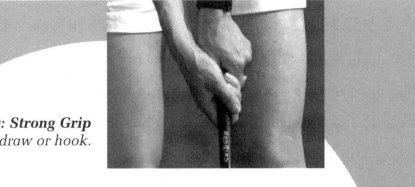

Figure 10: Strong Grip
Produces a draw or hook.

GRIP
ALIGNMENT

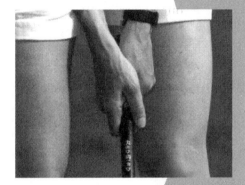

Figure 11: Neutral Grip
Can produce a straighter shot.

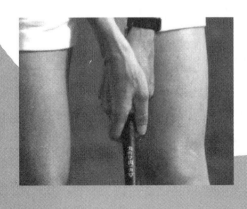

Figure 12: Weak Grip
Helps create a fade or slice.

ADDRESS

Your feet should be about shoulder-width apart with the 1-wood—measure this stance from the outside of your shoulders to the *inside* of your feet. Make sure you have an accurate perception of how wide your shoulders really are. Many people misjudge this! Hold a club across your chest and, using your index fingers along the shaft, mark the width of your shoulders. Carefully put the club on the ground, lining up the insides of your feet with your fingers to get an accurate measurement of the size of your shoulders. **(Figures 13A and 13B)**

Moving your feet a maximum of half an inch for each consecutive club, make slight adjustments with your stance depending on the club's length: with the shorter irons—8, 9, and the wedges—your stance narrows; and with the longer irons—1, 2, 3, 4, and the woods—it gets progressively wider, until it reaches the maximum of shoulder-width with the driver.

Imagine standing with a clock face underneath each foot. Point your right foot straight up to 12 o'clock, and toe your left foot out to about 11 o'clock. Divide your weight evenly between your feet.

The position of the ball between the feet has a great effect—on trajectory, clubface alignment at impact, and where in the club's path the ball is struck. Ball position at address is generally approached in two ways, and both end up with it played somewhere between the center of the stance and the left heel:

1. Play the ball in the same position regardless of the club used. For instance, Jack Nicklaus (among others) plays the ball the same distance off his left heel for every standard full swing. He widens his stance by moving his right foot for the longer clubs. This is an easy-to-remember, simple method.

2. This one is a little more involved: reposition the ball in the stance, depending on the club. With the longer clubs play the ball closer to

Figure 13A: Measuring shoulders for stance.

Figure 13B

Figure 14:
Spine angle
at address.

the left heel, then gradually move the ball toward the center of the stance as the clubs get shorter. Change the ball position by a half inch or less for each consecutive club.

Experiment. Only experience will tell which of these methods is best for you.

With your back fairly straight—don't slouch!—lean forward from your hips, enough that the front of your shoulders hang out one to four inches past your toes. **(Figure 14)** It may feel as though you're going to fall over when tilting your spine that far

forward, so stick your rear end out to feel better balanced. Setting your spine at this angle improves your swing in three important ways: First, your spine is aligned at the same angle it needs to be in at impact for solid contact with the ball. Second, sixty percent of your weight is across the balls of your feet, making it easier to shift your weight through impact. (That still leaves forty percent of your weight back on your heels, so don't tiptoe at address.) Third, with your spine in the correct position, your *relaxed* arms hang straight down from your shoulders and away from your legs, allowing plenty of room for your hands and arms to get by on the downswing.

If you're standing at address with an erect spine, you're prepared to play a different sport—baseball. Because a baseball batter is ready to hit a ball that's three feet off the ground, this upright spine is a major reason that beginning golfers hit topped shots, and even miss the ball completely. You must lean forward to reach the golf ball on the ground.

Now flex your knees. Imagine standing next to an eight-foot-high platform. If someone dropped a bag of golf clubs into your arms from the top of the platform, how much knee flex would be required to catch them? Experiment with more or less flex until you find a comfortable position. Keep your knees flexed throughout the swing—whether swinging your golf clubs or catching them, your legs should be prepared for some work.

At address your left shoulder, left arm, and the club shaft should form a straight line down to the ball. **(Figure 15)** This puts your hands opposite the inside of your left thigh, where your left hand is even with, or just past, the ball. The club's shaft should be leaning slightly toward the target. Notice we are discussing a face-on—<u>not</u> a down-the-line—view. Looking down the line, there should be a definite angle formed between your freely hanging arms and the club shaft. **(See Figure 14, previous page.)**

Figure 15

Once you're in the correct address position—spine tilted forward, knees flexed, weight balanced on the balls of your feet, and arms hanging straight down from your shoulders—plug the club into your hands. Voila! That's how far you should stand from the ball. As the clubs get longer, stand farther away from the ball; with a shorter club in your hands stand closer to the ball—but the basic address position remains constant. Standing too far from the ball doesn't allow your arms to hang straight down; you won't be relaxed while reaching out. Or stand too close to the ball, with your arms bent at the elbows and resting too close to your legs, and there won't be enough room to swing your arms past your legs, distorting the path of your swinging club.

Aiming and Alignment

When Tom Watson, Nancy Lopez, or any good golfer sets up to the ball, each follows a precise routine. This routine starts with establishing the *target line*—the imaginary line drawn from the ball to the target. The target line is an important reference point for the set-up; the clubface will be perpendicular, and you will be parallel, to it.

Align the clubhead to the target line before positioning your body: ignoring the top edge of the club, place the bottom-most leading edge of the

Figure 16A:
Accidentally aiming
to the right.

Figure 16B:
Correct alignment—
parallel left.

clubface perpendicular to the imaginary line the ball will travel out on. This points the face of the club directly toward the target at address, which is where it should be facing at impact.

Now align your body to the target line. At address, imaginary lines drawn across your toes, knees, hips, and most importantly your shoulders, should parallel the target line. Shoulder alignment is the most critical because your arms tend to swing out in the direction your shoulders are aiming, no matter where the rest of your body is pointing.

To check your alignment, start by laying a club on the ground across your toes. Now step behind the ball and look straight down the target line. Is this club on the ground parallel to the target line? Or is it pointing directly at the target? You should align your feet *parallel left* of the target line. If the line across your toes points toward the target, you aren't set up parallel to the line of flight. You are actually aiming off to the right. **(Figure 16A)**

Once your feet are aligned properly, arrange your knees, hips, and shoulders. **(Figure 16B)** Set them all parallel to the line across your toes. (Some golfers lay the club across their heels rather than their toes to get a clearer picture of the alignment of their feet; this avoids any ambiguity created by toeing their left foot out to 11 o'clock at address.)

FOLLOW-THROUGH

A balanced and relaxed follow-through is the result of all the good things happening before it. Shift your weight, uncoil, swing at a manageable tempo and stay relaxed during your swing, and you can't help but get to the timeless follow-through seen on golf magazine covers.

Many new students wonder why the follow-through is so important. They wonder why it would matter what their finishing position looks like when they have already hit the ball. Well, it turns out that the better your position is at the end of your swing, the better your impact position will be—learn the correct finish and the middle part greatly improves.

Because the follow-through, like the address, is a static position, it is easy to perfect. Once learned, you won't have to think about it during the swing.

Here are the components of the follow-through, along with a very quick method to make it part of your swing: **(Figure 17)**

❖ Finish with ninety-five percent of your weight on your left side. Most pros have so much weight on their left foot that they have rolled to the outside edge of their shoe—the spikes under the inside edge of the ball of their left foot are usually visible.

Figure 17:
The follow-through.

❖ Your shoulders and hips (that is, your belt buckle) point at the target, not to the right.

❖ Your right foot points straight down into the ground, with no bend in your toes. With bent toes, ninety-five percent of your weight hasn't really shifted onto your left foot. Think of that weight as potential distance and consistency left behind; it's not helping to move the club toward the target.

❖ The bottom of your right shoe faces straight back, away from the target.

And your knees should be fairly close together.

❖ Your spine is erect, with your shoulders directly above your hips. Don't lean either away from the target or toward it—that added pressure on your lower back can cause injury.

❖ Both arms have folded and your (relaxed) hands are past your left shoulder, with the club extended down your back.

Here's *the* drill to learn the follow-through quickly:

After every swing, check your follow-through. Make any adjustments that are necessary to attain the ideal position described above, then count to five, *slowly*. For example, if at the end of the swing your hips are pointing to the right, fix your position by aiming them toward the target. And maybe, because of a death-grip, the club is pointing straight up into the sky at the finish; relax your hands and allow the club to hang down your back. After fixing these problems, count to five deliberately, standing in the perfect position. Hold this flawless position for the full count to receive two important benefits:

1. Muscle Memory Your mind and body will quickly become comfortable

**Remember,
*Garbage in—
Garbage out*!**

with this new position; every time it's held, you are rehearsing and remembering. Because of muscle memory, your body starts to seek out this picture-perfect position without any conscious effort. And each time you hold this position, you are reinforcing the follow-through of the swings to come. (Muscle memory, a term used throughout this book, is a convenient shorthand for the *mind's* ability to digest, absorb, then recreate some of the positions in the golf swing. It absolutely does not mean that the muscles themselves have this ability.)

Remember, *Garbage in—Garbage out*! This saying applies to muscle memory as well as to computers. Put yourself in an incorrect follow-through, hold it for five seconds, and you will train your body to malfunction. Take care to make sure *everything* is perfect before starting the count.

2. Balance Notice how long the pros hold the follow-through position after impact. Most often they drop their arms and hands to their sides as the club and their arms recoil forward, but their lower body stays rooted in place. These players have had a good follow-through since age seven, so they are not posing like statues to develop muscle memory. What concerns them is being balanced at impact. They know that when they achieve a balanced end to their swing they are balanced throughout, and that means more shots on the sweet spot. Put another way: when amateur golfers are falling-down-out-of-control in the follow-through, they've lost their equilibrium at impact, too. Many poor shots result because they are swinging too hard and fast—at a pace they can't handle.

Now that we have talked about the positions to start and end with, let's look at the parts in-between.

WEIGHT SHIFT

All sports that involve the arms either throwing or swinging use the shifting of weight as a huge source of power. The weight is loaded up away from the target first, then dynamically shifted back toward the target using the lower body to start the forward motion. Consider Major League baseball, for example. The pitcher transfers all of his weight to his back foot during the wind-up and, using his legs and hips, powerfully throws that weight forward to start the delivery. Likewise, a baseball batter waits for the pitch with his weight loaded on his right foot. Then, driving his lower body forward, he shifts his weight aggressively toward the approaching ball. And how about football, tennis, racquetball, handball, boxing, or bowling? They all involve shifting weight toward the target,

propelling the arms, or whatever the hands are holding, toward the target.

Golf is no different. Unfortunately, the *automatic* weight shift of other sports feels anything but when we swing a golf club. Give almost anybody a baseball and, correctly, their natural inclination is to shift their weight to their right foot as they swing back, then throw their weight toward the target to propel their arm forward. There is very little weight on their right foot at the end of the throw. Compare that to what often happens with a golf club in their hands: their legs tend to sit there while they race their arms and hands to the ball in an attempt at generating clubhead speed. Often they actually fall *away* from the target in their follow-through. Imagine boxing and throwing a punch while your weight shifts away from your opponent. You won't generate much power that way.

In golf, you must learn to shift your weight effectively. During the backswing, make it your goal to transfer seventy-five to eighty percent of your weight away from the target, loading it onto your right foot. It's helpful to move your weight to the right immediately at the start of the backswing, rather than getting near the top of the backswing, then shifting. Take care of it right away and it's done.

This is a good time to lay to rest one of the great myths about the golf swing—Keep Your Head Perfectly

Still! Your friends are trying to be helpful when asserting this, but they have not been watching the best players in the world. This advice makes it nearly impossible to shift your weight back properly. When watching a professional golfer's backswing, a *slight* motion of his or her head to the right is evident. This small movement—usually not more than a couple of inches—is enough to get most of their weight loaded up behind the ball. It's no coincidence that someone throwing a football or baseball also moves their head to the right during the backswing. Essentially, that's why the weight shifts away from the target. (The turning of the left shoulder back during the golf swing also helps displace the weight to the right.)

Now we've come to one of the most important, and difficult, projects in the golf swing: using the *lower body* to initiate the downswing. This may sound strange, but even though the club is held in your hands, your lower body must create the power. Using your legs and hips to start the downswing allows the club to approach the ball on the proper path and generates maximum clubhead speed. If, on the other hand, the downswing starts with your hands, arms or shoulders, some typical golf disasters are produced—hooks, slices, topped shots, or the dreaded shank—all because of the detrimental effect your upper body has on the path, speed, and alignment of the clubhead.

Why is it so hard to use our legs properly in the golf swing? Unlike sports such as baseball or tennis, where we are reacting to a ball coming at us, in golf the ball is just sitting there waiting to be hit. We have all the time in the world to build up thoughts like: "I'm going to knock the cover off this ball," or "I'll send it to the moon!" It's this *"kill it"* mentality that causes the upper body to pull down from the top of the backswing before the lower body. We often sense during our worst swings that we're swinging so hard we might come out of our shoes. Conversely, some of our best shots feel like we didn't do anything—like cutting butter with a hot knife. Not coincidentally, that's the way we describe the swings of many of our favorite pros on TV.

Remember these four simple rules of weight shift and you won't have any trouble:

1. Start the backswing with an immediate shift to the right.

2. Start the downswing with your lower body.

3. Don't start the downswing with your upper body.

4. Repeat #2 and #3 above.

You can find specific triggers to make your legs more active during the downswing in **Leg Drive, page 36.**

FOUNDATIONS

The right leg and the spine—these are the two foundations of the golf swing that make it possible to return the clubhead back to the ball in the same place it started.

The Spine

For consistent ball striking, your spine must remain tilted forward at the same angle from address until well after impact. A slight change in the spine's position shifts the path and plane of your swing, making a solid shot more a matter of luck than anything else.

To understand the role of your spine, use your imagination: picture a wagon wheel, about nine feet in diameter, laying on its side, parallel to the ground. This wheel is resting on top of your shoulders with your head and neck poking through the hub (your spine takes the place of the wheel's axle). Tilting your spine forward until the wheel touches the ground at the ball puts you in the correct address position. **(Figure 18)** At this point your shoulders are hanging out past your toes one to four inches, and sixty percent of your weight is across the balls of your feet.

Notice when your shoulders turn at right angles around your spine, the club traces out parts of the wagon wheel. The shaft moves roughly in the same plane occupied by the spokes of the wheel, and the clubhead travels along the rim. For the club to return consistently to the ball, i.e., where the wheel touches the ground, your spine must remain steady, like an axle. Movement of your spine from its beginning position causes the wagon wheel to go with it. Lifting your spine before or during impact pulls the club away from the ball, causing thin and even completely missed shots.

For example, standing up during the backswing puts you in the same position a baseball batter takes while waiting for a pitch. Now the wagon wheel is parallel to the ground again, setting you up to swing at a ball three feet off the ground. Stee-rike! You just

Figure 18:
*The wagon wheel—
the shape of the
golf swing.*

missed the golf ball. The same thing happens when lifting your spine at impact.

Your spine should move from its original position into an erect one only well *after* impact, around the time your right arm becomes parallel to the ground. **(Figure 19)** Your right shoulder coming in contact with your chin swivels your head to the left, and finally lifts your upper body into the follow-through. Keep the angle of your spine tilted forward through most of your swing to play like a golfer, not a baseball batter.

Now, let's take a look at the other foundation for the golf swing—your right leg.

Figure 19:
Spine doesn't lift until after impact.

The Role of the Right Leg (Backswing)

The right leg contributes to the swing in two important ways: (1) Power—turning the shoulders fully against a braced right leg; (2) Consistency—a steady right leg provides a stable platform to swing around.

Coiling—Power

In the golf swing, your right leg acts like a spring: turn your shoulders fully on the backswing and your hips also have to turn. Practically your whole body is coiling onto your right leg, winding it up. As it uncoils through impact, this spring-like action of your right leg releases the stored tension, supplying tremendous power.

To get the most out of your right leg while taking the club back, shift your weight and coil your shoulders fully to the *inside* edge of your right foot; don't allow your weight to shift to the outside. Pointing your right foot straight up to twelve o'clock at address has prepared your right leg to accept and store this coil. It's too easy to take your weight to the outside of your right shoe when your foot points out to, say, two o'clock. Rolling to the outside edge of the right foot diminishes the coil, and with it, potential power.

Try this: take your address position (without a club) and lift the outside of your right foot off the ground enough to put a copy of a golf magazine under it. Keep your spine steady and turn your shoulders fully on the backswing, until your back is facing the target (or until your left shoulder moves behind the ball, or covers your right foot). Don't let the outside edge of your right foot touch the ground. Holding this top-of-the-backswing position, your right leg (somewhere between your knee and hip) should feel tight and fairly uncomfortable. That's the coil! If your leg doesn't feel taut and wound up, you haven't turned your shoulders enough or you've rolled to the outside of your right foot. Another way to lose the coil is to let your right knee straighten on the backswing. Then your leg becomes immobilized—it can't be used to uncoil during the downswing.

Coiling—Consistency

From hip to foot, your right leg should remain virtually still all the way up to the top. It's the bedrock of your backswing. Your hips should turn, coiling on the way back, but there should be a minimum of lateral movement. Especially watch your right hip: don't let it slip to the right. A sliding right hip produces a different range of motion every swing—moving two inches one time, and four inches the next—leading to highly unpredictable results.

Study **Figure 20** to the right. At the top of the backswing, notice that the line along a pro's back leans away from the target, while the line along the outside of the right leg leans toward the target (the same angle that the right leg started in at address). These two lines indicate a potential for maximum power—they illustrate a completely coiled backswing. Practice this top-of-the-backswing position in front of a mirror daily. Align yourself correctly, then hold this pose for 10 to 30 seconds. Muscle memory greatly speeds the time it takes to incorporate this position into your swing.

Figure 20:
Two powerful angles.

Hip Coil

There are two completely different, yet valid, schools of thought concerning the role of the hips during the coil. Note that they both incorporate a braced right leg:

1. Initiate the backswing with a hip turn. A full hip turn allows for a deeper coil and takes the club through a bigger arc, generating more clubhead speed.

2. Limit the hip turn during the backswing. This creates tremendous torque with the shoulders turning as far as they go against a restricted lower body.

Leg Drive

Although the right leg should remain as still as possible to achieve maximum coil during the backswing, don't confuse this with the downswing, where it needs to be very active.

Learn to uncoil your right leg by driving with your lower body *before* your arms and hands start down. This needs to be a powerful, dynamic move and it's one that most of us don't find natural. In fact, this is one of the biggest differences between the best players in the world and the average golfer. Most pros do little work from their waist up. Their arms, shoulders, and hands are relaxed, and on the downswing they don't have an abrupt acceleration from their upper bodies. But their legs are very aggressive on the downswing—it's the leg drive, releasing the coil and shifting the weight back toward the target, that is supplying the power in the golf swing. Most people at your local driving range are swinging much differently, with maximum tension and effort in their hands, arms, and shoulders, while their legs just sit there.

Those same people would never throw a baseball or football that way: they would be relaxed, with their motion toward the catcher dominated by the drive of their lower body. They would not *consciously* do anything with their legs—their lower body would work naturally, without any thought. Unfortunately, most of us can't rely on our legs to work the same natural way with a golf club in our hands. We need to make them move.

That's why even the best golfers in the world use a mental key—a "trigger"—to get their lower body to initiate the downswing.

For example:

Right Knee: Curtis Strange drives his right knee dynamically toward the ball and into the follow-through position. He calls it a *kick*, because he wants it to be an aggressive and powerful action. As his knee moves toward the ball, his right heel lifts off the ground along with the outside edge of that foot. This adds up to an ideal position at impact—right knee kicked in, right heel off the ground, outside of the right foot off the ground (even up by the little toe), the only part of his right foot touching the ground is the inside edge of the right big toe. At impact, ninety percent or more of his weight is on his left side.

Hips: One of Greg Norman's downswing keys has been to turn his hips powerfully toward the target. With his right hip—and quickly—he tries to replace the spot his left hip occupied at the top of his backswing. Nick Faldo uncoils his left hip straight back, behind his body. Keeping his hips "within his feet," he strives to turn them within the area of his stance on the downswing, avoiding an excessive sliding of his left hip toward the target. **(Figure 21A)** Done properly, his left leg doesn't buckle out toward the target through impact. **(Figure 21B)**

Plant Left Heel: Jack Nicklaus initiates his downswing by planting his left heel, simultaneously driving off the inside of his right foot.

Left Knee: Some good golfers start the downswing by driving their left knee toward the target.

All of these methods set off a chain reaction starting at ground level. No matter which trigger is used, the downswing sequence ultimately starts with the feet. Pushing off the inside edge of the right foot causes the left knee to move toward the target and drives the right knee toward the ball. The lower body uncoils, with the hips turning back toward the target and pulling the shoulders along, as the weight shifts back to the left. The shoulders then tug on the arms and, finally, the club is pulled down to the ball. This chain reaction consistently guides the club on the correct path through impact and generates considerable clubhead speed. You feel little effort, yet the ball goes higher, straighter, and farther.

All of this means the pros have little choice as far as the follow-through is concerned. Their leg drive forces them into that classic position at the end of their swings. On the other hand, pulling down with your hands, arms, and shoulders from the top of the backswing with dead legs produces the standard hacker's position at the end: out of balance, and right foot firmly planted on the ground, with too much weight remaining on it. Start thinking of that extra weight on your right foot as lost distance and consistency.

Here are two drills for your legs:

1. Short of seeing yourself on film, this drill is about the only way to tell for sure if your lower body is initiating the downswing, instead of your arms and shoulders. Take your backswing and stop at the top. Holding your upper body still, make the initial move down with your hips or

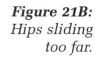

Figure 21B:
Hips sliding too far.

Figure 21A:
Correct hip turn.

legs, then stop again for a second or two. Now allow your arms to come down. Take at least 5 seconds to complete this drill—this isn't the fluid, smooth swing you'll eventually want. For many, this will be the first time they feel their lower bodies starting the downswing.

2. This drill reinforces the timing of the leg drive and ties the whole downswing together. Stop at the top of your backswing. Imagine your shoulders, arms, and hands are one solid, connected unit. Without using your arms and shoulders, *slowly* turn your hips and push off your right foot, shifting your weight into the follow-through—your belt buckle aimed toward the target, your right foot on the toes, and the bottom of your right shoe facing away from the target. Emphasize your weight shifting toward the target, not down at the ball, and avoid an excessive lateral slide of your hips toward the target. Try to feel your upper body being pulled down *solely* from the action of your lower body. Keep your spine at a constant angle to get the most from this drill. Practice these slow-motion swings without a ball at first. Then try it with a golf ball. Take the same slow swing without any thought about distance or direction; just try to get a sense of your legs doing the work.

Here are three reasons the average golfer does not use his or her legs:

1. They have never heard about the importance of the leg drive in the golf swing.

2. They *did* read about it somewhere. They tried it for a couple of shots, and it felt awful; they quit and went back to their old swing.

3. They tried it—but not only did it feel terrible, their good, and even mediocre, shots disappeared.

Now that you can't use the first excuse, try to get past the last two. I have given many lessons where a student's swing improved at the same time their shots got worse. But because of the newness of the instruction everything started to feel foreign and uncomfortable, and their shots deteriorated. Then, desperate to hit a good shot, they abandoned the new swing thoughts in favor of their old comfortable swing. The ball flight improved, but their swings got worse—and most importantly, they were back in their old positions where they were before the lesson started.

The key is to focus on the swing, and not where the ball goes. Take a lot of practice swings, without worrying about ball flight. When actually swinging at a ball work on the correct positions, ignoring ball flight at first. Soon it will start to feel natural. As you become comfortable with the new moves, you won't have to think about them as much; the shots will start to impress you, *and* your swing will have reached a new level.

SWING PATH

Inside-to-Down-the-Line

Consider the imaginary wagon wheel again, first mentioned under **The Spine, page 33.** Standing at address with your spine tilted forward, the wheel lays across your shoulders, perpendicular to your spine; the lowest part of the wheel's rim rests on the ground where the ball would be. Remember, the clubhead should follow the same path the rim takes. The rim of the wagon wheel is a road map for the swinging clubhead.

Let's call the side of the target line you are standing on the *inside;* and the other side of the line the *outside.* Notice how the rim/clubhead takes a path inside the target line as it approaches the ball, and how at impact the clubhead and the wheel's rim move directly down the line toward the target. **(Figure 22)** If the clubface is square (the bottom edge of the clubface perpendicular to the target line) at this point, a straight shot will result. With the ball target-bound, the clubhead and wheel rim move back inside the target line and up into the follow-through. This inside approach of the clubhead as it nears the ball is anything but exotic. It's a completely natural effect of swinging in a big circle (the wagon wheel) around your spine. (This correct path for the clubhead is often mistak-

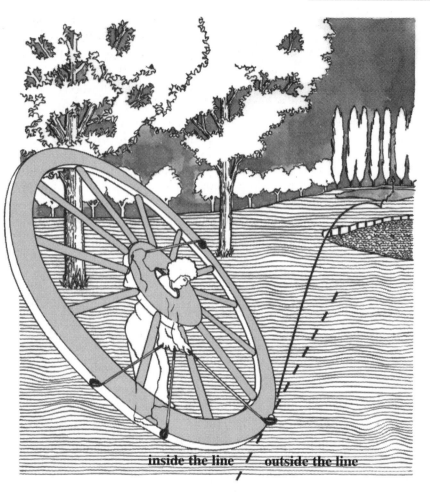

inside the line / outside the line

enly called *inside-to-out*, meaning inside the target line through impact, then back outside the line into the follow-through, because that's what it feels like. We can see *inside-to-down-the-target-line-to-back-inside* would be a much more accurate description of the proper path.)

For the club to approach the ball from inside the target line, start the

Figure 22:
Correct approach of clubhead through impact.

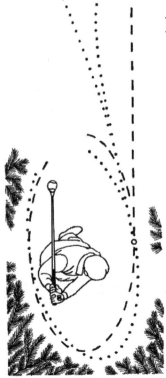

Figure 23:
*The physics behind
our mis-hits.*

downswing with your lower body, keeping the angle of your spine constant until well after impact. Your turning hips pull your s h o u l d e r s   around the axis of your spine, and cause your right elbow to tuck in close to your right side. Because your elbow stays close to your right hip, your hands drop down, also bringing the clubhead down, and to the inside of the target line.

Again, we can see how important a role the lower body plays in the golf swing.

Path—Outside-to-In

Reversing the correct sequence—starting the downswing with your upper body instead of your legs—causes the clubhead to end up outside the target line, cutting across the ball on its way back to the inside. The clubhead is swinging *outside-to-in*. This swing path produces shots at both ends of the spectrum—slices that curve out of control to the right, and pulls that go straight left. At this point, the resulting shot is mostly a matter of where the clubface is pointing at impact.

Find out if (like most people) you are swinging on this incorrect outside-to-in path. Get in the habit of asking yourself three questions after every swing:

1. Where is my shot starting?

2. Where does it finish?

3. What does that tell me as far as clubface alignment and swing path?

To answer the first question, keep this in mind: our shots tend to *start* their flight in the same direction the club's shaft is traveling at impact. To answer the second, the shots *finish* where the club's face points as it strikes the ball.

For example, an outside-to-in swing path with the clubface pointing to the right of the target (open) causes the ball to start left, but the shot ends up curving to the right. This is called a pull-slice. Striking the ball with that same outside-to-in swing path and the clubface aiming farther to the left (closed) causes the ball to start left and curve even farther left—a pull-hook. As you can see, the answers to numbers one and two above supply the clues for question number three. **(Figure 23)** We swing outside-to-in because our upper bodies are too active. Our shoulders, hands, or arms make the first downswing move. For example, *casting* can distort the path of the clubhead. Like casting a fishing line, our hands and arms move away from our body as our wrists uncock prematurely, throwing the clubhead outside the target line. Another way to swing outside-to-in is to *come over the top*—starting the downswing with the shoulders causes the right shoulder to move out toward the ball, taking our hands and arms along, throwing the clubhead outside the target line.

SWING PLANE

In his classic book, *Five Lessons— The Modern Fundamentals*, Ben Hogan gives a graphic depiction of the swing plane. He hired Anthony Ravelli, the preeminent golf illustrator, to sketch a 20-foot rectangular sheet of glass, leaning from the ball onto a golfer's shoulders. The golfer's head poked through a hole near the top of the glass, with the bottom edge of the pane resting on top of the target line. The idea is to keep the club moving along the glass without pulling away from it, or crashing through it, during the swing. When the club moves outside the target line on the backswing, it breaks the glass. On the downswing, the club will probably take the same outside-to-in route, crashing through the glass again as it approaches the ball, resulting in either a pull or a slice. See **Swing Path, page 39**. Ironically, when the club moves in the opposite direction on the way back, pulling inside away from the glass, it can still crash through the glass on the way down, because in an attempt to get back on the correct path our shoulders, arms, and hands can loop, *coming over the top* and causing an outside-to-in path. The loop occurs because our overactive upper body causes the right shoulder to move out toward the ball. That takes our hands and arms along and throws the clubhead outside the target line.

Figure 24:
Different sized bodies produce different swing planes.

Figure 25B:
Shaft of club parallel to the target line and ground.

Although Hogan used the glass, it might be helpful instead to think of a wagon wheel **(The Spine, page 33)** as defining your swing plane. The proper angle for the wheel to rest against your shoulders is dictated by your address position, as well as your build. We all have slightly different swing planes—it's definitely not the case of one size fitting all. Generally, taller golfers are more upright, and shorter players have flatter swing planes. **(Figure 24, previous page)** Whatever your size, when the shaft of the club moves along the spokes of the wheel, it is on plane. Start the takeaway with the clubhead following the rim of the wheel and stay that way up to the top of the backswing, and an on-plane position is likely at impact.

Here are some checkpoints for your swing plane during the backswing. . .

1. Guard against *laying the club off*—pointing it behind you. **(Figure 25A)** When your club is parallel to the ground halfway back, it should also be parallel to the target line. **(Figure 25B)**
2. The ends of the shaft should point to the target line at all stages of the swing, except when the club is

parallel to the ground. Imagine the target line stretching out to infinity in both directions. During the backswing, the clubhead-end of the shaft should point along the target line to your right, until the shaft is parallel to the ground—that's at about hip level. After this point, the grip end of the shaft should point at the target line to your left, toward the target. From there, the grip-end should continue tracking the target line back to, and past the ball, until the club is again parallel to the ground at the top of your backswing. **(Figure 27, top of next page)**

Figure 26

. . .for the swing plane at the top of your backswing. . .

3. Your right upper arm, the part your biceps attaches to, should be parallel to the ground; it, and your right forearm, should resemble a ninety-degree angle, like the letter 'L'; your right elbow should be under your hands. **(Figure 26A)**

4. The line your left arm forms should <u>not</u> be below the plane of your shoulders. Someone standing behind you, looking past your ball down the target line, should see your left arm on a steeper plane than your shoulders. **(Figure 26B)**

5. Your hands are higher than your head **(Figure 26C)**, because your left arm will be at a steeper angle than your shoulders, and because your upper

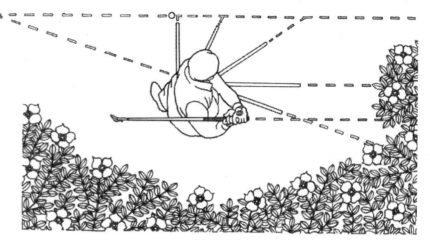

right arm is parallel to the ground.

6. At the top, an equilateral triangle (approximately) formed by the forearms and right shoulder and biceps should be visible **(Figure 26D)**. The triangle's bottom edge should be parallel to the ground because the upper right arm defines it. (# 3 above.)

. . .and on the way down:

The clubhead should feel like it stays behind your body for much of the downswing. It should feel like someone standing beside you, looking past your ball out to the target, would see the clubhead stay to the outside (to the left) of your rear-end until it reaches about hip high (depending on how long the club is—with a longer club the clubhead stays outside your body farther into the downswing). **(Figure 28)**

Figure 27:
The shaft points to the target line for most of the swing.

Figure 28

CLUBHEAD SPEED

Clubhead speed equals distance. That sounds logical and innocent enough. But in that one statement lurks the root of much of the evil in the golf swing. Most people intuitively sense they need clubhead speed to produce longer shots, and they try to swing their arms and hands as fast as possible to create it. Surprisingly, this tends to produce exactly the opposite effect—the faster the average golfer swings his or her arms, the *slower* the clubhead moves through impact, and actually results in a loss of distance.

> ... the faster the average golfer swings his or her arms, the *slower* the clubhead moves through impact, and actually results in a loss of distance.

Here's why:

Clubhead speed is directly linked to the two hinges in your swing:

1. Your shoulders turning around your spine. A full shoulder turn takes the club through a bigger arc, building more clubhead speed on the way down **(see Coiling, page 34)**.

2. Your wrists hinging on the backswing and unhinging through impact. They more than double the clubhead speed supplied by the turning of your shoulders.

Take a super-relaxed grip on one of your clubs and swing slowly until you reach the top of the backswing. Notice how your wrists cocked naturally without any effort on your part. Relaxed hands allowed your wrists to hinge up on the backswing in response to the weight and momentum of the club. Then they unhinge down by the ball because centrifugal force pulls the clubhead out away from the center of the swing. Both momentum and centrifugal force are universal—and *external to* your body. They work the same way swing after swing, if allowed to. On the other side of the coin, you have little chance of consciously controlling your wrists during impact—not when an average swing lasts 1.3 seconds and the clubhead travels between 80 and 120 miles per hour.

Because of the momentum-caused hinging of your wrists at the top of the backswing, your left forearm and shaft of the club should form roughly a ninety-degree angle. This angle should remain intact on the way down to the ball, almost until the moment of impact—the so-called *late hit.* **(Figure 29)** Maximum clubhead speed is achieved when centrifugal force finally unhinges your wrists for you, forming a straight line down your left arm and the shaft of the club. Here's another way to put it: a fraction of a second before impact, the hands are within five inches of the position they will be in when the club strikes the ball. Yet at this point, the shaft of the club should be almost parallel to the ground with the clubhead still three to four feet from the ball. In the split second it takes to get from this position to impact, the hands move a few inches, while the clubhead has to move four feet to strike the ball. In order to catch up with the hands, the clubhead has to travel much faster over a greater distance. This "late" hit produces clubhead speeds in excess of 100 mph.

Remember that we are talking about clubhead speed, not arm speed. Watch Nancy Lopez, Fred Couples, Payne Stewart, Larry Mize, and Beth Daniel. Their arms do not move 100 mph: in fact, they aren't moving their arms nearly as fast as many of the amateurs at your range. Yet they are able to hit the ball twice as far, and twice as accurately.

Casting

Unfortunately, most golfers at the driving range do not have a late hit. At the top of the backswing, the thought, "I'm going to send this straight to the Moon, Alice—to the Moon!" pops into their head. Their arms and hands instantly tighten, allowing them to pull down abruptly

Figure 29:
The Late Hit.

on the club. Just like throwing out a fishing line from a rod and reel, they *cast*—their wrists immediately start to uncock on the way down. Remember, maximum clubhead speed is reached when the wrists unhinge. Casting causes the maximum speed to occur too early, at least two feet before the club reaches the ball. Now the clubhead is really decelerating through impact.

Here's another way to look at it: when casting, the left forearm and the shaft of the club form a straight line too soon. Now the clubhead is trapped at about the same speed the left arm is traveling. Your left arm will not be moving a hundred miles per hour

Correct Impact Position

through impact, and neither will the club. Lack of clubhead speed, and therefore distance, is only one effect of this problem.

Consider the other difficulties caused by casting:

1. Fat shots. In a pro's swing, at that split second before impact when the hands are almost even with the ball, the clubhead is still about hip high—two feet off the ground. **(Figure 29, previous page)** When an amateur is casting, at that same moment the clubhead might only be a fraction of an inch off the ground. **(Figure 30)** Fat shots, with the club-

Figure 30

head hitting the ground behind the ball, are a distinct possibility.

2. Thin shots. Subconsciously, when we cast we are trying to get the clubhead to the ball before anything else, including our wrists. Picture an impact position where the clubhead leads and the hands trail: the club's shaft leans back away from the target because the clubhead has passed the hands. **(Figure 31)** From here the clubhead has to move up as it passes the hinge of the wrists, resulting in topped (thin) shots.

3. Because the clubhead is getting to impact prematurely, the clubface tends to square up

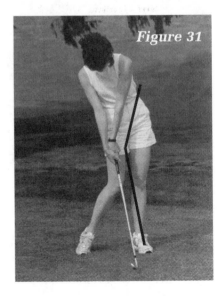

Figure 31

Final Tips on Clubhead Speed

❖ <u>Don't</u> increase your grip pressure to hold the ninety-degree angle between your left forearm and the club shaft into the downswing. Your wrists will lock up and they won't be able to unhinge freely. Sam Snead, one of the longest hitters ever, has said many times that his wrists feel *oily* when he plays his best golf: they hinge and unhinge without restriction.

❖ One day someone may suggest that you manipulate your hands during your swing, that you cock your wrists and uncock them consciously. My advice is to forget it. When you consider the speed of the clubhead, and the short duration of the swing, how can you time out your wrist action to the exact moment of impact? You can't. And neither can anybody else.

❖ One key to generating clubhead speed is leg action. Start your downswing from the ground up. Your lower body will pull your upper body—cocked wrists and all—down in one piece. Inertia helps to keep your wrists properly hinged by holding the clubhead back, until centrifugal force unhinges your wrists down by the ball.

During your next range visit, you'll probably notice someone swinging their arms as fast as possible and wondering why their ball barely gets off the tee line. These same golfers will say that some of their longest, straightest shots occur when they feel as if they are barely swinging their arms—everything feels effortless. Now you know why.

sooner than it should, pointing to the left of the target as it strikes the ball. The ball could easily hook from there.

4. With a good swing the hands lead the way to the ball and, after impact, centrifugal force pulls the clubhead out toward the target. When casting, the clubhead passes the hands before impact and the blade starts to move upward instead of out. This creates pressure on the left arm, causing it to collapse and acquire the classic *blocking* look. **(See pages 51 to 53.)** For most amateurs this blocking action usually overcomes the problem in # 3 above, causing slices and/or thin shots instead.

We are rushing our upper bodies down to the ball in a misguided attempt at generating clubhead speed and, instead of powerfully straight shots, we cause every problem in the (this) book. I repeat: arm speed alone *does not* create clubhead speed. Relaxed wrists—hinging and unhinging freely—*do*.

Figure 32A

HOW YOUR ARMS SHOULD FOLD

During The Backswing

Your right arm should fold naturally on the way to the top. It might bend early in the backswing, like Bernhard Langer or, like Jack Nicklaus, it may start to fold much later. No matter when your right arm folds, at the top of the backswing it should take roughly the same position it would be in when carrying a tray of drinks: (a) your upper arm—your biceps—should be parallel to the ground; (b) your right elbow is below your hands, supporting the club like you would a tray; (c) your right arm takes on the look of the letter 'L', close to being a right angle. **(Figure 32A)**

Watch out for a *flying* right elbow at the top—with the forearm parallel to the ground, and the elbow above the shoulders, not under the hands. **(Figure 32B)** This problem can lead to casting, by causing your right arm to straighten during the downswing, pushing your hands and the clubhead away from your body. Also, with the club immediately getting off the swing plane and outside the target line, the clubhead cuts across the ball at impact, creating pulls and slices. **(See Swing Plane, page 41.)**

Much has been said about the role of the left arm in the swing. Many self-appointed experts at the range will warn you, "Keep your left arm stiff and straight on the backswing!"

Let me set the record—not your left arm—straight.

While it is true that some (*very* few) of the pros keep their left arms perfectly straight, the rest allow some bend on the backswing. Betsy King is

Figure 32B

one of these rare exceptions. Look at her arm during her backswing—it's actually hyper-extended. Betsy King is double-jointed: she has the ability to keep her left arm perfectly straight as well as relaxed. However, watch Nancy Lopez or Curtis Strange, or just about anybody else: their left arms bend. But they don't bend much.

Many amateurs have an excessively bent left arm—almost to ninety-degrees—at the top. **(Figure 33)** This shortens the arc of their swing with a loss of distance resulting. Also, it's

Figure 33

unlikely they'll reach impact with their left arm in the same extended position it was at address: centrifugal force won't have enough time to pull their left arm back out away from the center of their swing by then. With their left arm bent at impact in the classic blocking position **(Figure 37A, page 52)**, they top the ball, slice it, or a combination of the two.

The bottom line with the left arm: Keep it as straight and firm as possible during the backswing—*as long as it's totally relaxed*. Staying relaxed allows centrifugal force and a complete release to straighten that arm by impact.

For a firmer left arm at the top:
❖ Surprisingly, you can improve your left arm by fixing your right. Put your right arm into the shape of the letter 'L' at the top of the backswing, and your left arm automatically firms up. **(Review Swing Plane, #3, page 43.)**

❖ Try to keep your hands the same distance from your shoulders—at address, during the backswing, and down through the ball. Imagine a string attached at one end to the grip of the club, and at the other end to a button on your shirt. With the imaginary string taut at address, keep it that way throughout the backswing and into the follow-through. A limp string anywhere during the backswing means your left arm is collapsing, and your hands are coming closer to your shoulders.

During The Downswing

The first movement during the downswing should be from your lower body, for reasons already covered. As your hips turn to face the target, they tug on your shoulders and pull your arms down. As your hands reach about hip-high, your left arm is firm and straight, not locked or tight, with your right elbow tucked in close to your right hip, helping to establish the proper inside swing path. **(Figure 34)** Likewise at impact, your left arm has remained extended; your right arm should still be slightly bent with the elbow close to your right hip.

Just after impact is the only point in the swing where both arms extend fully. Then, as your hands reach about hip high, your arms start to reverse their roles: your left arm bends slightly, with the left elbow staying close to the side of your upper body. **(Figure 36A, next page)** Your extending right arm remains firm, yet relaxed, as your hands move up past the level of your shoulders. Stay relaxed into the follow-through, and both arms will begin to bend naturally when they are roughly perpendicular to the ground, with your hands nearly above your head. At the end of your

Figure 35

swing, your arms will have folded completely, your hands should be near your left shoulder, and the club will be wrapped around your back. **(Figure 35)**

So far I've been talking about sections or pieces of the arm swing. Keep in mind that the pros are not thinking of these as separate positions. They use single swing keys to make their arms flow properly throughout the downswing. We'll look at three of these keys in the next section.

Figure 34

RELEASING

When your arms work correctly through impact, as described above, it's called *releasing*. **(Figure 36A)** Releasing is often illustrated in golf magazines and books by showing the toe of the club pointing straight up when the club shaft is parallel to the ground, halfway into the follow-through. **(Figure 36B)** To achieve this toe-up position, the clubface is turning as it squares up through impact. Releasing provides straighter shots and other benefits, including greater clubhead speed, and as the arms extend more at impact, the ability to compress the ball and take a divot.

Unfortunately, most golfers, and even the pros now and then, do not release properly. They *block.* Looking at **Figure 37A (next page)**, when a golfer blocks, the left arm has not folded properly, or soon enough, after the club strikes the ball. This classic blocked position—the left arm bowed out, leaving air between the left side and elbow—holds the clubface wide open (aimed to the right) as the ball is struck, and produces a slice. Looking now at a point halfway into the follow-through, notice the toe of the club points to the right instead of straight up—evidence of an open clubface at impact. **(Figure 37B)**

Blocking is also a great way to top the ball. Remember, we are trying to get our upper body back to virtually the same place it started from at address. With both elbows spread apart in this blocked position at impact, the clubhead is being lifted away from the ball and a thin shot is likely. Look around at the range and watch the vast majority of golfers either topping the ball or slicing it to the right. It's no coincidence that most of them are also blocking.

Figure 36B:
*Toe up—
a released
clubhead.*

Figure 36A:
The Release.

☝Figure 37B:
Open club-
face.

Figure 37A:
Blocking

Here's a word of warning: sometime in the future a friend, or even a pro, might suggest that to keep from slicing the ball you should roll your wrists to the left through impact. I strongly advise against this, for two reasons: (1) Your wrists are a small part of your body and can move quickly—with an average golf swing lasting 1.3 seconds, exactly when do you time out the wrist-roll? (2) Your wrists can move with great variation. Try this: hold your right hand out as if you are about to shake someone's hand and keep your forearm still. Notice the ways your wrists can hinge: with your little finger moving closer to the ground; with the back of your hand coming closer to your forearm; and with your thumb turning to left. Adding to the problem, your wrists can move with a combination of these actions, and to varying degrees. There is too much possible movement to control consistently, especially during the fastest part of the swing.

Instead, here's how many pros release their arms:

❖ From elbow to wrist, roll your forearms counterclockwise through impact. This is a great move to work on because it forces your arms to work correctly through the ball. Your left arm folds naturally with your elbow pointing down at your side as your right arm extends. The clubface turns along with your forearms, squaring up as you hit the ball. Because of the speed and short duration of the swing, you may have to think about rolling your arms at the beginning of the downswing, instead of at the ball. It's like a delayed reaction: think about turning your forearms immediately on the way down, and they won't really start turning until impact.

❖ Here's a second method from Tom Watson: touch your forearms together at your wrists when your right forearm is parallel to the ground, halfway into the follow-through. When trying this method of releasing, keep four things in mind: (1) Watson tries to get his arms to touch down by his wrists, not half way up his forearms; (2) Because he has forearms similar in size to Popeye's, he doesn't have much trouble getting them to touch—if you are shaped anything like the rest of us, your forearms might not be big enough to actually touch, but try to get them as close as possible; (3) They only touch, or come close to touching, for a fraction of a second, when your right arm is parallel to the ground just after impact; (4) Don't let your left wrist break down through the ball; avoid any kind of scooping action from your hands. Imagine attaching a ruler under the watch band on your left wrist: because the ruler sticks out on both sides of the watch, it keeps your left wrist in line with your left forearm. **(Figure 38)**

❖ And a third method from Nick Faldo: imagine hitting a Ping-Pong ball left-handed. Hit a backhand, top-spin smash, while keeping your upper left arm, from shoulder to elbow, close to the left side of your rib cage through impact.

All of these swing keys cause your arms to move in the same ways—for example, when rolling your forearms through impact they touch (or come close) in the follow-through. Alternately, when you get them to touch, your forearms will have rolled through impact.

Figure 38:
Ruler keeping the left wrist flat.

CONNECTION

Have you ever heard of connection? A one-piece takeaway? Or turning the triangle of your arms and shoulders away from the ball to start your backswing? These are all different ways of saying exactly the same thing. They have to do with tying smaller parts of your body, your hands and arms, into a larger part, your shoulders, during the swing. When connected, your shoulders, arms, and hands start back away from the ball in one piece; and they stop at the top of your back-swing at the same time. (Refer to Jimmy Ballard's fine book, *How to Perfect Your Golf Swing*, for more information about connection.)

Power is increased when you acquire connection: now your shoulders coil fully against a braced right leg because your whole upper body is turning in one piece up to the top of the backswing.

Uniting your arms and shoulders together throughout the swing also has a great effect on your consistency. Because your shoulders tend to move at right angles to your spine, putting them in control of the takeaway cuts down on excess movement—an economy of motion. Or to put it another way: your disconnected arms are free to move with great variation, drifting away from your body and taking the club outside, or conversely, too much to the inside, on the back-swing. All this extra movement leads to inconsistent results.

Use the following to improve your connection:

❖ Try to keep your sternum (breast-bone) pointing at your hands throughout the backswing. Because of the folding right arm it's only possible to do this until your hands reach about hip-high, but it's a good idea to try to feel as though you're doing it all the way up to the top. Here's a drill that can help: Take your normal address with a 7-iron, but put the butt-end of the club up against your sternum.

Figure 39:
The triangle.

Extend your arms in their usual position, but let your hands slide down the shaft onto the metal. Your arms and shoulders now form a triangle: with the base defined by your shoulders, your arms define the sides, and the apex of the triangle represented by your hands. **(Figure 39)** Notice how your shoulders point straight down the shaft toward your hands. Without letting the grip-end of the club come away from your sternum, keep this triangle intact on the backswing until the shaft of the club reaches parallel with the ground and your hands are about hip high. When your shoulders point down the club shaft at your hands, your back faces the target—you are coiled and connected.

❖ Keep your upper left arm and chest (your left armpit) 'plugged' together, all the way to the top and down through impact, until about when your hands reach hip high into the follow-through. It helps to hold something like a golf glove or head cover under your left armpit during your swing. **(Figure 40)** Don't let it come out until well after impact.

❖ Move the triangle formed by your arms and shoulders away from the ball in one piece. Feel your shoulders taking your arms back, not the other way around.

Figure 40:
"Connecting" your left
arm to your shoulders.

DIVOTS

Most amateurs would guess that the pros hit their irons so high because the clubhead gets under the ball, lifting it up. In truth, something very different is happening—the clubhead actually moves down as it strikes the ball, compressing it into the ground, *with the ball rebounding up into the air.* It doesn't sound logical at first, but here is the evidence that will convince you:

Figure 41:
Divots—product of a downward blow.

Divots Not only are the pros taking divots on almost every shot, they are taking them in front—*to the left*—of the ball. When hitting a good shot, the clubhead is approaching the ball on a downward path and, after the ball is struck, the clubface continues down, taking out the grass in front of where the ball used to be. **(Figure 41)**

(By taking the divot behind the ball, a pro would experience the same results as the rest of us: the clubhead would be slowing down as it digs through the ground on its way to the ball, and the clubface would be twisted in the wrong direction. You can't take the divot out in front of the ball correctly when trying to hit up on the ball.)

Spin The next time you watch golf on TV, look for a wedge shot that hits the green, then— as if being jerked with a string— spins back in the direction of the golfer. This backspin is created when the grooves of the clubface grab onto the ball as it is being pinched against the ground. Look at the size of the divots coming out of the ground during these swings. They aren't that deep, but they can be very long with a lot of surface area. On the other hand, can you see that if the club really moved up at impact, the ball would float toward the green with very little backspin, then roll *away* from the golfer?

Can't Get Under It This finally convinced me that I had to learn to hit down: If you want to hit the ball with the sweet spot—which is very near to the center of the clubface—how do you get that part of the club under the ground to be able to hit up on the ball? You can't, because the ground is in the way. About the only thing you can do is hit the ball thin, because the leading edge of the clubface will be moving up at impact.

Keep in mind that the divots you see the pros taking are not deep gashes coming out of the ground. They are just barely hitting down. But the difference between barely hitting down and barely hitting up is like night and day in terms of how high and far your shots travel.

By the way: if when working on this you suddenly start hitting fat shots, take it as a sign of progress. You are learning to give the ball a descending blow, but you haven't practiced long enough to be able to hit the ball first, then the ground to the left of it.

ODDS AND ENDS

Pre-Shot Routine

Shot to shot, day in and day out, the best golfers in the world repeat the same pre-shot routine each time they step up to the ball. They do it in such an exacting way that it doesn't vary by more than one second! Watch the pros on TV to see them following precise, *personal* pre-shot routines for their full swings, and with slight variations, their short shots. Betsy King's full swing routine is simple— she aligns her feet, glances at the target, fine-tunes her stance, and then she swings. Other golfers have more complex methods. For example, Jack Nicklaus, after aligning his body to the target line, takes a couple of big, slow waggles, checks the target a few times, takes one more waggle, cocks his chin to the right and, finally, firms his left arm. That last step triggers his backswing. Although it varies from player to player, every pro goes through his or her same routine, every swing.

Pre-shot routines serve many functions:

❖ A routine performed hundreds and even thousands of times breeds confidence. Even under pressure, a pre-shot routine surrounds you with familiar actions and positions. A personal routine is reassuring and soothing, and helps relieve any anxiety you may feel—even when standing over a three-foot putt to win a fifty-cent bet.

❖ A pre-shot routine keeps your muscles in motion, helping you stay relaxed and loose. Coming to a complete standstill before the start of the swing can cause you to tighten up. Some golfers have trouble taking the club away from the ball because they don't have a pre-shot routine to move through. They get stuck over the ball, never coming to the part of the routine that says *GO!* The timing of their takeaway changes with each swing—often they start the backswing with a sudden jerk, and when they aren't really ready.

❖   A routine provides the time and a method to align your feet, knees, hips, shoulders, and clubface properly at address. **(See Aiming and Alignment, page 27.)** Without taking the time to aim, you could hit one of the best shots of your life exactly where you were pointing— out of bounds, in the lake, or into someone's back yard.

❖   Visualizing a successful result is sometimes the only thing that separates a good shot from a bad one. On the other side of the coin, think about the times you stood over the ball and talked yourself into hitting it poorly. Golf shots often turn out *exactly the way you see them in your mind before the swing*. During your pre-shot routine, use visualization to program positive results. Before taking the club back, spend a few seconds getting a clear picture in your head of the swing, the flight

of the ball, and the landing spot. See the entire shot—and as vividly as possible. Jack Nicklaus calls this "going to the movies," and he uses visualization before every shot, even at the range; Ben Crenshaw never putts without first *seeing* the ball roll along the green, before dropping into the cup.

SAMPLE PRE-SHOT ROUTINES

Routine A

1. After selecting the club, stand behind the ball and look straight down the target line. Fix the line vividly in your mind to be able to set your body and club relative to it.

2. Walk up to your ball and align the clubhead behind it, pointing down the target line. Then take your grip on the club.

3. Put your right foot in roughly its final position: pointing at 12 o'clock, and the correct distance from the ball. During this step you are measuring to the ball (how far to stand from it), with your spine tilted forward and arms hanging totally relaxed, straight down and away from your legs.

4. Move your left foot up so that your toes are parallel to the target line, with your feet roughly shoulder-width

apart and the ball played somewhere between the middle of your stance and your left heel. Now square up the rest of your body—knees, hips, and shoulders.

5. Settling down into the finished address, take one to four slow, relaxed waggles. A waggle is essentially a movement of the clubhead away from the ball. Done with your wrists or shoulders (usually a combination of both), it's used as a way to relax your hands and forearms, and as a rehearsal for the takeaway. For example, you can help to groove a one-piece takeaway by waggling the triangle formed by your shoulders and arms. The clubhead can move back and forth three inches or three feet, but settle on a comfortable range of movement and keep it the same every time. Choose between one and four waggles, but always take the same amount before each shot.

6. After the last waggle, take one more look at the target, then pull the trigger and start your backswing.

Routine B

1. Repeat '1' above, but as you look down the line, point the club toward the sky and take your grip before walking up to the ball. In this routine, your grip goes on the club first before putting the clubhead behind the ball. **(Figure 42)** Now place the clubhead behind the ball.

2. Repeat '3' above, except this time step up to the ball with both of your feet together, side by side. Even though your toes are only an inch apart, align them parallel to the target line. **(Figure 43, next page)**

3. Spread your feet to about shoulder-width, with the ball between the middle of your stance and your left heel. Keep your toes parallel to the target line while doing all of this.

4. Repeat '5' and '6' above.

Figure 42:
Pre-shot routine with grip going on before alignment.

These are just two of the many pre-shot routines out there. To develop your own, watch the pros on TV and steal (borrow) one of their routines, move by move. Or modify one to fit your needs. Practice and develop your routine at the range—this helps prevent rushing through the bucket of balls, and is also a great way to improve your powers of concentration.

Use the same basic routine for the full swing, pitching, and bunker shots. Modify that routine slightly—to include reading the green, etc.—to use for putting and chipping. But find a routine for *all* your shots.

Practice Swings

Most good golfers take one or two practice swings before they hit a full swing shot. But watch closely—they usually aren't taken at normal speed. It's often a much slower motion, and sometimes doesn't even include a club. Here's why:

❖ Less wear and tear on the body. It takes your golfing muscles at least 45 seconds to recover from an all-out practice swing. Without waiting long enough after the practice swing to hit the ball, your muscles won't be at one hundred percent, and something will be taken off the shot—either accuracy, distance, or both.

❖ A golfer taking two full practice swings before each shot can poop out by the 12th hole. The golfer with slow-motion rehearsal swings has a greater chance to play the finishing holes well, with more energy and better concentration.

❖ Unhurried practice swings encourage a more controlled swing at the ball, and a better leg drive. Most golfers notice their best shots come from leisurely, effortless swings. Think of your slow-motion practice swings as dress rehearsals for the real thing.

Figure 43

◆ ◆ ◆ ◆ ◆

CHAPTER THREE

FULL SWING PROBLEMS AND SOLUTIONS

Look up your specific problem shot, find the appropriate subheading, and try the bulleted cures until you find the correct fix.

INCONSISTENCY

You aren't alone if you've ever left the golf course mumbling something about being so inconsistent. Inconsistency is everyone's complaint, even the pros'. A professional golfer rarely wins back-to-back tournaments—they might take home the winner's check one week and miss the cut the next.

When plagued with unwanted hooks, slices, and missed putts during a tournament, pros head for the range immediately after signing their score cards. They aren't looking for exotic cures; they're checking and adjusting the basics of a sound swing—grip, address, alignment, weight shift, etc. No magical quick-fix for inconsistency exists. Your progress takes time and depends on diligent practice.

❖ Go to the range regularly. With *proper* practice, the more balls you hit the more consistent you become.

❖ Here's one of the best and simplest ways to gain consistency: for two to five minutes a day take practice swings with your clubhead *touching the ground*. Practice this at home (use an old carpet or welcome mat) or at the range, but don't swing at any object—no whiffle ball, leaf, cigarette butt, or anything else. At first make sure the club touches the carpet or mat exactly where the ball would be in your stance. As you improve, learn to hit a spot just to the left of the ball. **(See Scooping, page 78; Divots, page 56.)** This drill teaches the eye-hand coordination that is absolutely necessary to become consistent.

❖ Buy your own set of clubs. Consistency is hard to come by when borrowing clubs from friends or renting a different set every time you play and practice. Consider buying custom-made clubs that a professional fits to your needs—shaft length, grip size, lie angle, etc. **(See Buying Clubs, page 165.)**

❖ Establish a pre-shot routine. You can't expect consistent results without a consistent set-up. Practice your pre-shot routine at the range, paying particular attention to alignment and ball position. **(See Pre-Shot Routine, page 57.)**

❖ Work on specific swing changes at the range, *not* on the golf course. Consistency comes from making the same correction over and over. What better place to do that than the range? Use this book to figure out where your inconsistency comes from, then refine your swing at the range; don't try to build a swing on the course, where each shot counts.

❖ Be consistent in the instruction you follow, too. Advice from your friends should make you wary; what works for them might not work for you. And half the time it's not working for them, either. Find a good teacher and follow his or her advice. Avoid jumping from teacher to teacher; all that differing advice leads to sensory overload. **(Page 16)**

❖ See your professional on a consistent basis to make sure you aren't slipping into bad habits. **(See page 16.)** Between lessons, the use of a mirror at home can supply instant feedback about your progress.

SHOTS TO THE RIGHT

TO THE RIGHT: SLICES

Ball starts straight, then curves uncontrollably to the right.

CLUBS
❖ When your missed shots travel low and to the right, your clubs could be too heavy or the shafts might be too stiff. **(See Buying Clubs, page 165.)**

❖ Hitting high and to the right could mean: (1) the shafts of your clubs are too flexible, or (2) with the woods, the clubface has an open angle built into it. **(See Buying Clubs, page 165.)**

GRIP
With your hands in a weak position (turned counterclockwise) at address, they will be square when they reach impact—but the clubface will be pointing to the right.
❖ Avoid a weak grip. Instead use a neutral or slightly strong grip, where the back of your left hand, and the palm of your right, point at the target or just to the right and above it. **(See page 23.)**

❖ Keep your grip pressure light in both hands, especially your left-hand grip pressure equal to your right. Too much grip pressure in your left hand holds the clubface open through impact, inhibiting the correct release of your arms and promoting a blocked shot to the right. Maintain that light and equal-to-your-right-hand feeling all the way into the follow-through. Imagine holding an opened tube of toothpaste, a stick of room temperature butter, or a live bird. Don't squeeze any of them. **(See page 21.)**

ADDRESS
The clubface should point toward the target at address to help ensure its return there at impact. Slicing can start with an open clubface at address—that is, with the clubface pointing to the right of the target.
❖ Square the club at address by setting the bottom leading edge perpendicular to the target line. Ignore the top edge. **(Aiming and Alignment, page 27.)**

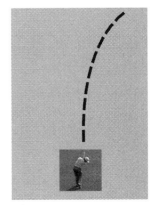

SLICE

Steve Juetten

Steve's **blocking** caused many problems, including: thin shots, slicing, and shots hit off the toe of the club. Most of his practice time revolved around learning to turn his forearms *very* early on the downswing.

Time Spent on Project:
17 Weeks

Average Score: 89

Practice Schedule:
2 to 3 times a Week

Playing Schedule:
Once a Week

Lowest Score: 79

Playing Since: 1992

Occupation:
Management Consultant

BLOCKING

Your arms are not releasing properly **(Figure 44)**, holding the clubface open at impact. **(See Releasing, page 51.)** Try three techniques to promote the correct release:

❖ Roll your forearms counterclockwise through impact from elbow to wrist. The clubface turns along with your forearms, squaring up when striking the ball. Stay relaxed to get the most from this drill.

❖ Try to touch your forearms together halfway into the follow-through, when your right forearm is parallel to the ground. Bring your arms together at your wrists, not up by your elbows. **(Figure 45)**

❖ While keeping your left elbow close to your side, turn your left forearm counterclockwise in exactly the same way you would to hit a left-handed, backhand, topspin shot while playing Ping-Pong. Keep your upper left arm against the left side of your chest through impact.

Figure 44

Figure 45

TO THE RIGHT: PULL SLICES

Ball starts left, then curves back to the right. Review **Slices, Page 63** *for the slicing part of the shot; see below for the pulling.*

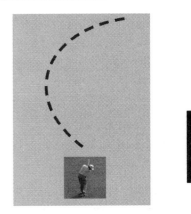

PULL SLICE

BALL POSITION
Because of the correct inside-to-down-the-line-back-to-inside path of the club through impact, the ball can start left when played too far forward in your stance.
❖ Play the ball farther back in your stance. Move it at most a quarter of an inch at a time as you experiment, and remember to keep it somewhere between your left heel and the center of your stance. **(See page 25.)**

ADDRESS
Check your alignment to make sure your body isn't aiming to the left.
❖ Set your toes, knees, hips, and shoulders parallel to the target line. Take your address position and keep your upper body as still as possible. With one hand by the clubhead and the other by the grip, slowly lift your club up and lay the shaft horizontally across your shoulders. It should be parallel to the target line. **(See Aiming and Alignment, page 27.)** Shoulder alignment at address affects the path of the club through impact. Your shoulders pointing to the left of the target line can cause your arms to swing on an outside-to-in path, leading to pulls. When you block at the same time **(see Blocking, previous page)**, the ball starts left, then curves back to the right—a pull-slice.

SWING PATH
The clubhead should approach the ball from inside the target line, travel down the line at impact, then return back to the inside after striking the ball. A pull results when the club tracks toward the ball from outside the target line. When combined with blocking **(see Slices, Blocking, previous page)**, this same path creates a pull-slice.
❖ Avoid laying the club off during the backswing. **(See Figure 25A, page 42.)** This can cause you to *come over the top*—where an overactive upper body causes the right shoulder to move out toward the ball, taking your hands and arms along and throwing the clubhead outside the target line.

❖ Initiate the downswing with your lower body to keep from coming over the top. Here are three ways to start the downswing properly: drive your right knee at the ball; turn your hips powerfully toward the target; drive your left

Figure 46:
The Three Ball Drill.

knee at the target. But above all, the first move on the downswing must be with your lower body. **(See page 36.)**

❖ As shown in **Figure 46 above**, put three golf balls down about two inches apart in a line set at a forty-five-degree angle to the target line. Practice hitting *only* the middle ball. To succeed, you are forced to swing the club from inside the target line as it approaches the ball, down the line at impact, and then back to the inside after the ball is struck. Because an outside-to-in swing can get all three balls moving at once, use this drill only when the person in the stall immediately to your right is adequately protected.

❖ Keep the clubhead behind your body as long as possible on the downswing. **(See Figure 28, page 43.)**

❖ Hit the inside of the ball. Rather than the whole ball, aim to hit a specific area of it—like the carefully positioned label or stripes. **(Figure 47, next page)**

❖ Casting can cause the clubhead to approach the ball on the wrong path (outside-to-in), leading to pulls. **(Fat Shots, Casting, page 85; Casting page 45.)**

❖ Take a cardboard box to the range. Lay it about 2 inches outside, and parallel to, the target line. As in **Figure 48**, line the ball up roughly in the middle of the side of the box. Try to hit the ball solidly without touching the box on either side of the ball. Don't pull away from the ball in an attempt to avoid the box.

❖ Stop at the top of your backswing. Imagine your shoulders, arms, and hands are one solid, connected unit. Without using your arms and shoulders to pull the club down, *slowly* turn your hips and push off your right foot, shifting your weight into the follow-through. Feel your upper body being pulled down— solely from the action of your lower body—as your wrists stay cocked.

Figure 47

Figure 48:
The Shoe Box Drill.

To get the most from this drill, keep your spine at a constant angle. Practice these slow-motion swings without a ball at first. Then try it with a golf ball. Take the same unhurried swing without any thoughts about distance or direction; just try to get a sense of your uncoiling lower body doing the work.

❖ EXPERIMENT: Although the clubhead should travel back to the inside of the target line after impact, try to propel it out to the right of the target through the ball. Pick a landmark out on the horizon to the right of the target, and swing the clubhead out toward that object through impact. Often— even though it can feel excessive— exaggerating a move like this during the swing will just barely produce the correct position.

PUSH

TO THE RIGHT: PUSHES

Ball starts and continues straight right.

CLUBS

❖ The lie angle of your irons is too flat. **(See Buying Clubs, page 165.)**

❖ The shafts of your irons are too short. **(See Buying Clubs, page 165.)**

ADDRESS

The lines across your toes, knees, hips, and shoulders should be parallel *left* of the target line—aimed slightly to the left of the target. **(See Figures 16A and B, page 28.)** When your body points directly *at* the target, the line parallel to your body and through the ball aims to the right of the target. Even with a perfect swing, your shot will be pushed to the right.

❖ After taking your address position, use an extra club as an alignment aid by laying it on the ground across your toes. Move to stand behind the club, looking down the line toward the target. That club and the target line should be parallel and *not* converge off in the distance. If they are not parallel, move the club to make it so. Now square up your toes, knees, hips, and shoulders to this correct reference point. **(See Aiming and Alignment, page 27.)**

❖ Make sure your shoulders are square to the target line, not pointing to the right in a closed position—your arms will tend to swing out in the same direction your shoulders are pointing, with the ball starting right. To check, take your address position and, while keeping your upper body as still as possible, slowly lift your club up and lay it horizontally across your shoulders. That club across your upper body should be parallel to the club across your toes on the ground. **(See above.)**

BALL POSITION

Because of the correct inside-to-down-the-line path of the club as it approaches impact, the ball can travel right when played too far back in your stance.

❖ EXPERIMENT: Move the ball forward in your stance and see if that helps. Don't move it more than a quarter of an inch at a time, and remember to keep it somewhere between your left heel and the center of your stance. **(See page 25.)**

Figure 49

Figure 50

Carmen Miller

Carmen's main concern was to quiet her spine movement. Using these drills, she was able to accomplish this in fairly short order.

Time Spent on Project:
9 Weeks

Average Score: 112

Practice Schedule:
Once a Week

Playing Schedule:
Once a Week

Lowest Score: 95

Playing Since: 1988

Occupation:
Online Industry
Consultant

HEAD AND SPINE MOVEMENT

Many of your worst shots, including pushes, can be caused by head movement—especially movement toward the target during the downswing. **(Figure 49)** Keep your head steady and behind the ball at impact. **(See The Spine, page 33.)**

❖ Imagine a metal pole running down your back and into the ground, keeping your spine in position at address and during the swing. **(See Figure 51, next page.)** As your shoulders turn, your spine should stay against this pole—until well after impact.

❖ Keep your forehead lightly touching an imaginary wall, from address until your right shoulder comes into contact with your chin after impact. **(See Figure 51, next page.)**

❖ Recreate and hold the perfect impact position for at least 30 seconds. Pay particular attention to keeping your upper body back behind the ball. This is a good drill to do in front of a mirror using **Figure 52, next page** as your guide. A couple of minutes a day increases your muscle memory for this position.

❖ Imagine a string attached from your right shoulder to the club shaft at the top of your backswing. **(See Figure 65, page 100.)** Keep the string attached during the downswing until your hands are near your right thigh. Do this drill with a steady spine to help keep your head behind the ball at impact.

DISCONNECTION

In a *connected* golf swing, your arms are linked to your upper body throughout the swing. When your arms *disconnect* from the bigger muscles of your shoulders during the backswing, they (and the club) are free to wander on the downswing. **(See Connection, page 54.)** This often returns the clubhead to the ball on the wrong path, in this case *inside-to-out*, causing a pushed shot.

❖ 'Plug' your left upper arm against your chest at your left armpit. Keep that area snug, but relaxed, throughout the backswing and until well after impact. **(Figure 40, page 55)**

Figure 51:
Forehead stays against wall; spine mimics pole.

❖ Cultivate the one-piece takeaway. Move the triangle formed by your arms and shoulders in one piece during the swing, especially on the way back. Don't let your hands and arms control the backswing—it should feel as though your shoulders take your arms, hands, and the club back.

❖ Starting with the clubhead slightly off the ground at address can also promote a one-piece, connected takeaway.

Figure 52:
Muscle memory— hold correct impact position.

TO THE RIGHT: PUSH SLICES

Ball starts right, then curves even more in that direction.
❖ Review Slices **(page 63)** and Pushes **(page 68)** individually above for each
   component of this shot.

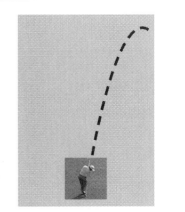

PUSH SLICE

TO THE RIGHT: SHANKS, WITH IRONS

*Shanks come from hitting the ball off the rounded hosel where the shaft enters
the clubhead. With the irons, this causes the ball to fly to the right to varying
degrees—anywhere from kind of right, to hitting the person in the stall next to
you.*

ADDRESS
You are standing too close to the ball when your spine is erect and your arms
hang against your legs. Using your lower body dynamically causes your arms—
and the club with them—to move out away from your body to get past your
driving legs. The hosel rather than the clubface impacts the ball, causing a shank.
❖ With your rear-end sticking out behind you, tilt your spine forward so that
   your shoulders are out 1 to 4 inches past your toes at address; make sure
   your arms are relaxed and hanging like pieces of rope, straight down and
   well away from your legs. **(See pages 25-27.)**

❖ Make sure you have positioned the club's sweet spot, not the hosel, behind
   the ball at address.

SHANK/IRONS

HEAD AND SPINE MOVEMENT
Head movement, especially toward the target during the downswing, can cause
shanking. Make sure your head stays behind the ball at impact.
❖ **(See Head and Spine Movement, page 69; The Spine, page 33.)**

BLADE OPEN AT IMPACT
When the clubface points severely to the right at impact, the hosel can be the
first part of the club to reach the ball. Both excessive left-hand grip pressure and
blocking hold the blade open at impact.
❖ Ease the tension of your left hand on the grip. Try for equally light grip pressure

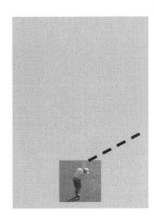

with both hands, from address to follow-through. Imagine holding an un-capped tube of toothpaste, a room-temperature stick of butter, or a live bird. Don't end up gripping a greased dead bird covered with toothpaste. **(See page 21.)**

❖ Roll your forearms counterclockwise through impact from elbow to wrist. The clubface turns along with your forearms to square up when striking the ball. Stay relaxed to get the most from this drill. **(Pages 51-53)**

❖ Try to touch your forearms together halfway into the follow-through, when your right forearm is parallel to the ground. Bring your arms together at your wrists, not up by your elbows. **(See Figure 45, page 64.)**

❖ While keeping your left elbow close to your side, turn your left forearm counterclockwise in exactly the same way you would hit a left-handed, backhand, topspin shot while playing Ping-Pong. **(See Releasing, page 51.)** Be careful to keep your upper left arm against the left side of your chest through impact.

DISCONNECTION
Disconnected arms can take the clubhead out away from the body at impact, lining the hosel up with the ball.
❖ 'Plug' your upper left arm against your chest at your left armpit. Keep that area snug, but relaxed, throughout the backswing **(Figure 40, page 55)** and until well after impact.

❖ Cultivate the one-piece takeaway. Move the triangle formed by your arms and shoulders in one piece during the swing, especially on the way back. Don't let your hands and arms control the backswing—it should feel as though your shoulders take your arms, hands, and the club back. **(See Connection, page 54.)**

SWING PATH
Cutting across the ball (outside-to-in) can line the hosel up with the ball at impact, causing a shank. **(See all cures under Pull Slices, Swing Path, page 65.)**
❖ Avoid laying the club off during the backswing. **(See Figure 25A, page 42.)** This can cause you to come *over the top*—where an overactive upper body causes the right shoulder to move out toward the ball, taking your hands and arms along and throwing the clubhead outside the target line.

TO THE RIGHT: OFF THE TOE

Striking the ball with the toe of the club causes the clubface to twist open, pointing to the right, and that's where the ball goes.

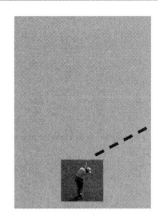

TOED SHOT

ADDRESS

❖ Spine too erect: with your spine in the same position as a baseball batter's while waiting for the pitch, the clubhead travels down the target line for only a moment during the swing. As the clubhead comes back inside the target line near impact, the toe catches the ball, sending it to the right. The cure: with your rear-end sticking out behind you, tilt your spine forward so that your shoulders are out 1 to 4 inches past your toes at address; make sure your arms are relaxed and hanging like pieces of rope, straight down and well away from your legs. **(See pages 25-27.)**

❖ Reaching: stretching your arms out toward the ball at address and then taking a good swing can cause your arms, and especially the clubhead, to pull in closer to your body (where they belong) on the downswing—so the toe of the club strikes the ball. Let your arms hang straight down and relaxed in your setup. **(See pages 25-27; Figures 61 and 62, page 96.)**

BALL POSITION

Because of the inside-to-down-the-line-back-to-inside path of a good swing, the toe of the club can strike the ball when the ball is positioned too far forward in the stance. **(See Swing Path, page 39.)**

❖ Move the ball back in your stance, a quarter of an inch at a time. Remember to play it somewhere between the middle of your stance and your left heel. **(See page 25.)**

HEAD AND SPINE MOVEMENT

Lifting your spine during your swing pulls the clubhead toward your body, causing the toe of the club to strike the ball. Watch out for too much drift from your upper body in these two places in your swing:

A. Backswing

❖ Turn your shoulders around the fixed axis of your spine, from the start of your swing through impact. In your address position, imagine a metal pole running down your back and into the ground, keeping your spine in position.

Keep your spine against the pole—not only during the backswing but until well after impact. **(See Figure 51, page 70.)**

❖ Imagine a wall built between you and the ball. The forward tilt of your spine at address places your forehead lightly against the wall. Keep your forehead against this imaginary wall throughout the backswing. **(See Figure 51, page 70.)**

❖ Imagine a sheet of glass above your head at address; don't allow your head to lift up into it during the backswing.

B. Impact

❖ Watch the ball until well after it's struck: keep your head in about the same position it started in at address, until seeing an empty spot where the ball used to be. **(See Figure 19, page 34.)** Then your right shoulder contacts your chin and lifts you into the follow-through; wait for your shoulder to swivel your chin to the left before taking your eyes off the spot where the ball was.

❖ Imagine a sheet of glass across the top of your head: don't break the glass by lifting your head. Don't lift your head to track the ball until your right shoulder hits your chin and carries you up into the follow-through position.

❖ Picture a wall built between you and the ball. Because of the forward tilt of your spine at address, your forehead touches the wall lightly. Keep your forehead against this imaginary wall through impact until your right shoulder comes into your chin. **(See Figure 51, page 70.)**

❖ Recreate and hold the perfect impact position for at least 30 seconds. Pay particular attention to keeping your upper body back behind the ball. This is a good drill to do in front of a mirror using **Figure 52, page 70** as your guide. A couple of minutes a day increases your muscle memory for this position.

BLOCKING

The correct release of your arms through impact returns them and the clubhead to almost the same position they started in. On the other hand, with elbows bent in the classic blocked position of many amateur golfers, the clubhead is pulled up away from the ball and toward you. Instead of the sweet spot, the toe of the club strikes the ball, sending it to the right. **(See Figure 44, page 64.)**

THIN SHOTS

We all know those low-flying shots that sting our hands and send the worms running for cover. Hitting the top of the ball with the bottom edge of the club causes these thin, or topped shots, and they are one of the most common ways to mis-hit the ball.

ADDRESS

Tilt your spine forward at address to solidly strike down on the ball. Many amateur golfers address the ball standing too erect. With their spines almost straight up and down, they are in the same position as a baseball batter—ready to hit a ball three feet off the ground. In other words they set up to swing *above* the golf ball, causing topped shots.

❖ Check your address position: with your back fairly straight, tilt your spine forward enough that your shoulders hang out beyond your toes. To check your position, lightly hold the grip end of your club between your index finger and thumb and let it dangle from your shoulders. When the shaft hangs over your foot or near your knees you are standing too erect. **(Figure 53)** The shaft should be hanging out between one and four inches past your toes. **(Figure 54)** To counterbalance the weight of your shoulders in this new position, stick your rear end out (more than you might think). **(Pages 25-27)**

Figure 53

Figure 54

Izetta Hatcher

Izetta hit many topped shots until learning to lean forward more at address. Like many people, she was standing too erect, preparing to swing a base-ball bat—well above the ground.

Time Spent on Project:
2 Weeks

Average Score: 97

Practice Schedule:
3 times per Week

Playing Schedule:
Twice a Week

Lowest Score: 92

Playing Since: 1980

Occupation:
Retired Registered Nurse

BALL POSITION

The clubhead must approach the ball at the correct angle to hit solid shots. With the ball played too far forward (left of center) in your stance, the club moves upward at impact, causing a thin shot.

❖ For iron shots: the club needs to be moving down and through impact, taking a shallow divot in *front* (on the target side) of the ball. **(Page 56; page 97)** Move the ball back in your stance, about a quarter of an inch at a time, until divots start coming out to the left of that spot. But be careful—unless intentionally trying to hit a low shot, avoid playing the ball to the right of center. That lessens the *effective loft* of the clubhead at impact. **(See Chipping, Setup, #2, page 127.)** Try to find the ball position that allows for hitting down and taking a divot, while still lofting the shots nicely into the air. For most people that's somewhere between the middle of their stance and left heel.

❖ With fairway woods you have a choice: try to take a divot (see bullet immediately above), or sweep the ball off the fairway. To sweep it, play the ball slightly farther forward in your stance, but not so much that it causes thin shots.

❖ When swinging a wood with the ball teed up: the clubhead should be traveling level with the ground, or slightly upward, at impact. Avoid playing the ball to the left of your left big toe. Playing the ball too far forward allows the clubhead to catch the ball as it moves upward into the follow-through, causing a topped tee shot. Position the ball somewhere between your left instep and one to three inches inside (to the right of) your left heel.

HEAD AND SPINE MOVEMENT

The best players keep their spines steady throughout the swing. Many amateurs lift their spines during the backswing and at impact, pulling the clubhead up and away from the ball. A thin shot results—unless the exact compensating downward move of their spine occurs as the club returns to the ball.

A. Backswing

❖ Turn your shoulders around the fixed axis of your spine, from the start of your swing through impact. In your address position, imagine a metal pole running down your back and into the ground, keeping your spine in position. **(See Figure 51, page 70.)** Keep your spine against the pole—not only during the backswing, but until well after impact.

❖ Imagine a wall built between you and the ball. The forward tilt of your spine at address places your forehead lightly against the wall. **(See Figure 51, page 70.)** Keep your forehead against this imaginary wall throughout the backswing and beyond impact.

❖ Imagine a sheet of glass above your head at address; don't allow your head to lift up into it during the backswing.

B. Impact

❖ Watch the ball until well after it's struck: keep your head in about the same position it started from at address, until seeing an empty spot where the ball used to be. Then your right shoulder contacts your chin and lifts you into the follow-through; wait for your shoulder to swivel your chin to the left before taking your eyes off the spot where the ball was.

❖ Imagine a sheet of glass across the top of your head: don't break the glass by lifting your head. Don't lift your head to track the ball until your right shoulder hits your chin and carries you up into the follow-through position.

❖ Picture a wall built between you and the ball. Because of the forward tilt of your spine at address, your forehead touches the wall lightly. Keep your forehead against this imaginary wall through impact until your right shoulder comes into your chin. **(See Figure 51, page 70.)**

❖ Recreate and hold the perfect impact position for at least 30 seconds. Pay particular attention to keeping your upper body back behind the ball. This is a good drill to do in front of a mirror using **Figure 52, page 70** as your guide. A couple of minutes a day increases your muscle memory for this position.

LOCKED KNEES

Flexed knees are an important ingredient in the golf swing. They not only encourage your lower body to generate power, but keeping them at a constant flex allows you to get back to impact with the clubhead at the same height relative to the ground that it started from. Straightening your knees before impact lifts the club away from the ground along with your body. Thin shots result.

❖ Take some swings without the ball. Stop at the top of your backswing and make sure your knees are flexed. Your right knee should be flexed to the same degree it was at address. Check your right knee on the backswing, and your left knee through impact and into the follow-through.

Tim Halm

Tim's **scooping** caused thin and fat shots, hooks, and a major loss of clubhead speed. This is a very difficult project for most golfers—the key for Tim was to learn to hit down on the ball, instead of trying to get under it to lift it into the air.

Time Spent on Project:
30 Weeks

Average Score: 85

Practice Schedule:
2 to 3 times a Week

Playing Schedule:
Once a Week

Lowest Score: 75

Playing Since: 1960

Occupation:
Physician

SCOOPING

Trying to get under the ball to lift or scoop it up gets the clubhead to the ball before your hands. **(Figure 55)** The clubhead should trail your hands **(Figure 56)** through impact—a late hit. **(Pages 44-47)** In the two Figures below, notice the differences in the positions of the hands. When your wrists remain properly hinged, the clubhead has not reached its lowest point—through impact it's still moving down. Trying to get under the ball has the opposite effect: because the clubhead has reached a point even with or past your hands, the only way for your clubhead to move is up. This scooping action puts the bottom edge of the club (as it moves upward) against the top of the ball, blading it. The following drills produce divots **(See Divots page 56; page 97)** in front of the ball instead.

❖ Think of pinching or trapping the ball between the clubhead and ground at impact. Nick Faldo calls it "squeezing the ball away." The point is to compress the ball between the clubface and the ground.

Figure 55   *Figure 56*

❖ Try to drive the ball down into a spot about half an inch to the left of the ball. Choose a spot right in front of the ball. **(Figure 57)** *Don't* lower your head and spine to accomplish this.

❖ Before each shot at the range, position the brand name or range stripe at the top back quarter of the ball . Picture the clubface pointing down as the sweet spot strikes that stripe squarely at impact. **(Figure 58)**

❖ Push a tee into the ground about an inch in front of your ball, leaving a quarter inch of the tee sticking up. Hit the tee after striking the ball and you'll be hitting down. When hitting off a mat, look at a spot a half inch in front of the ball; make sure your club strikes the mat there.

Figure 57:
Drive the ball down into the spot.

Figure 58:
Sweet spot hits the stripe.

BLOCKING

The correct release extends your arms through impact, helping return the club to ground level. Elbows bent in the classic blocked position of many amateur golfers pulls the clubhead up away from the ground. The bottom edge of the club, instead of the sweet spot, strikes the ball. **(See Releasing, page 51.)** Try three techniques to promote the correct release:

❖ Roll your forearms counterclockwise through impact from elbow to wrist. The clubface turns along with your forearms to square up when striking the ball. Stay relaxed to get the most from this drill.

❖ Try to touch your forearms together halfway into the follow-through, when your right forearm is parallel to the ground. Bring your arms together at your wrists, not up by your elbows.

❖ While keeping your left elbow close to your side, turn your left forearm counterclockwise in exactly the same way you would hit a left-handed, backhand, topspin shot while playing Ping-Pong. Keep your upper left arm against the left side of your chest through impact.

SWING PLANE

The correct swing plane delivers the clubhead into the ball at the angle necessary to hit down, taking divots. We all have slightly different swing planes—generally, taller golfers are more upright, while shorter players have flatter swing planes. Start the takeaway on plane, stay that way up to the top of the backswing, and an on-plane position at impact becomes routine. An excessively flat swing plane causes topped shots—like a baseball bat, the club will be above the ground at impact. **(See Swing Plane, page 41.)**

SWING PLANE—ADDRESS

❖ Check your address position; standing too erect flattens the swing plane. With your back fairly straight, tilt your spine forward so your shoulders hang out between one and four inches beyond your toes.

SWING PLANE—THE BACKSWING

Here's a quick review of the imaginary wagon wheel sketched out in the Full Swing Basics section **(Pages 39-43)**. Standing at address with your spine tilted forward, the wheel lays across your shoulders, perpendicular to your spine; the lowest part of the wheel's rim rests on the ground where the ball would be.

❖ Remember, the clubhead should closely follow the same path as the rim of the wheel—downward as it approaches the ball. **(See Figure 22, page 39.)** Take practice swings with this in mind.

❖ Guard against *laying your club off*—pointing it behind you. **(See Figure 25A, page 42.)** This flattens the swing plane. Take some slow-motion practice swings without the ball. Stop the club at exactly the moment it becomes parallel to the ground on the backswing. At this point the shaft should also be parallel to the target line. If it's not, fix it and hold this correct position for a count of ten and repeat. Muscle memory helps ingrain this position.

❖ To stay on plane, one end of the club shaft should point to the target line throughout the swing, except when the club is parallel to the ground. Imagine: (1) the target line stretches out to infinity in both directions, and (2) there are tightly focused flashlights inserted in both ends of the shaft of your golf club. Keep one of those beams shining on the target line during every part of your swing, except when the shaft is parallel to the ground and the target line. When taking the club back, the clubhead-end flashlight should point along the target line to the right until the shaft is parallel to the ground— that's at about hip level. Then as the club continues back, the grip-end beam should point toward the target line to the left of your ball. From there it should continue tracking the target line back to, past, and then to the right of the ball, until the club is again parallel to the ground at the top of the backswing. **(See Figure 27, page 43.)**

Swing Plane—the Top

Stop at the top of your backswing. Using the figure on the next page, check these positions:

❖ Your right upper arm—shoulder to elbow—should be parallel to the ground; your upper arm and forearm should approximate a ninety-degree angle, similar to the shape of the letter 'L', with your right elbow under your hands.

❖ At the top, there should be a hollow, roughly equilateral triangle formed by your upper body. When viewed from behind, your right shoulder, upper arm, and elbow form the base and your forearms create the sides of this triangle. Because your upper right arm defines it, the triangle's bottom edge should be parallel to the ground. **(See bullet above.)**

❖ Note that your shoulder plane is not parallel to the ground—because your spine is tilted forward, your right shoulder is higher than your left in the backswing. The plane of your left forearm arm should *not* be parallel to your shoulder plane. Someone standing behind you, looking past your ball down the target line, should see your left arm on a steeper plane than your shoulders.

❖ Your hands will be higher than your head, because the plane of your left arm is more upright than your shoulder plane and your upper right arm is parallel to the ground.

FAT SHOTS

Fat shots occur when the clubhead hits the ground before striking the ball. Most of us have experienced shots where the divot travels farther (and sometimes straighter) than the ball. Or maybe we've hit so deeply behind the ball that the divot flopped over and completely covered the ball. While thin shots sting your hands, fat shots can sting your pride.

EYE-HAND COORDINATION

One of the simplest and most effective ways to stop hitting fat shots is to learn to hit the same spot on the ground over and over again—and that spot needs to be to the left of the ball, not behind it.

❖ For 2 to 5 minutes, take practice swings using a 6-iron without a ball. Stay relaxed and swing slowly. On every swing try to hit the same *exact* spot on the ground slightly to the left of where the ball would be. Many amateurs, even experienced players, are mildly shocked to see how difficult this can be at first.

ADDRESS

Good golfers strike the ball with their upper bodies in nearly the same position they started from at address. Head, spine, shoulders, arms, hands, club shaft, and clubhead return to just about where they began before taking the club back.

❖ Clubhead Position—put the clubhead no more than a quarter of an inch behind the ball. Begin with your club too far behind the ball—by two or three inches, say—and at impact it can end up right back where it started, producing a fat shot.

❖ Ball Position (with the irons only)—the club makes solid contact with the ball just before the lowest point of its swing arc. For this to happen, the ball needs to be properly positioned. Playing the ball too far forward causes the club to hit the ground behind the ball. Take some practice swings without the ball, looking for the exact spot where the clubhead makes contact with the grass or mat. Put your ball 1/4 inch to the right of that spot, allowing for solid contact with the ball first, then the ground. **(See Divots, page 56.)**

EXCESS MOVEMENT OF THE SPINE AND HEAD

It's almost impossible to keep your head perfectly still, but you should strive to keep its up and down travel to a minimum. With your head lower at impact than it was at address, the club can bottom out before hitting the ball. Here are three common places in the golf swing where your head may be dropping, with the cures following each:

1. Lifting your head on the backswing, then overcorrecting on the downswing, which causes your head to drop lower than it started from at address.

❖ Pretend a metal pole runs down your back and into the ground, keeping your spine in position at address and during the swing. **(See Figure 51, page 70.)** With your shoulders turning, your spine should stay against this pole until well after impact.

❖ Imagine a sheet of glass above your head at address; don't allow your head to lift up into it during the backswing.

❖ Keep your forehead lightly touching an imaginary wall at address and throughout the backswing. Don't let your head pull away. **(See Figure 51, page 70.)**

2. Dropping your head on the backswing and leaving it there while striking the ball.

❖ Picture a metal pole (the same one in #1 above) extending along your spine and down into the ground, keeping your spine and head fixed in position. Without a ball, practice turning your shoulders around that axis. Hold a club across the back of your shoulders and try to keep it perpendicular to your *steady* spine during this drill. Do this in front of a mirror for better feedback.

❖ Imagine your chin is resting on top of a table at address, keeping your head from dipping during the backswing.

❖ Keep your forehead lightly touching an imaginary wall at address and throughout the backswing. Don't allow your head to push into the wall. **(See Figure 51, page 70.)**

3. Dropping your head on the downswing. If this is your problem, you are probably starting down by pulling on the club with your upper body, instead of using your lower body to uncoil and shift your weight toward the target. As your arms and shoulders pull the club down, your head follows, bringing the club to a lower position than it started from at address.

❖ Put more emphasis on starting the downswing with your lower body. **(See Leg Drive, page 36.)** Try each of these triggers for your first move down from the top of your backswing:

1. Kick your right knee in toward the ball.

2. Turn and clear your hips—specifically your left hip—powerfully toward the target.

3. Plant your left heel while driving the weight off the inside edge of your right foot.

4. Drive your left knee toward the target.

❖ You are less likely to dip your head on the downswing when driving with your legs instead of using your arms and shoulders. Practice this drill without a ball, in super slow-motion, and keep your spine and head steady from start to finish. Take your backswing and stop at the top. While holding your back toward the target for as long as possible, slowly move your lower body through impact and into the follow-through position—your belt buckle aimed at the target, your right foot on the toes, and the bottom of your right shoe facing away from the target. Can you feel your uncoiling legs and hips pulling your arms down toward impact? Emphasize your weight shifting toward the target, not down at the ball. Be careful with your hips: uncoil them by turning, not by sliding your left hip laterally toward the target.

❖ Keep your forehead lightly touching an imaginary wall at address, throughout the backswing, and especially on the downswing. Don't allow your head to push into the wall. **(See Figure 51, page 70.)**

CASTING (SCOOPING)

When *casting*, the wrists unhinge too early in the downswing, and the clubhead reaches its lowest point sooner than it should. Your chances of hitting the ground behind the ball skyrocket. With a *late hit*, the clubhead is a couple of feet away from the ground when the hands have almost reached the ball. **(See Clubhead Speed, page 44.)** The clubhead is moving down as the wrists unhinge, with the ball being struck first, then the ground.

❖ Use your upper body less. Instead use your hips and legs to start the downswing to help keep your wrists cocked longer. **(See the previous page, top bullet.)**

❖ **Review Hinging and Unhinging of Wrists, bottom of page 98.**

❖ Learn to take a divot in front of the ball with your irons. You are much less likely to cast when hitting down, taking the turf out to the left of the ball. **(See Scooping, page 78; Divots, page 56.)**

❖ At the top of your backswing, imagine a string attached from your right shoulder to the club's shaft directly above your shoulder. **(See Figure 65, page 100.)** This string holds the shaft close to your shoulder on the downswing until your hands are hip-high, keeping your wrists cocked much longer.

❖ Try to hit the ball with the club's shaft in a straight line with your left arm and wrist. The shaft should be leaning *toward* the target at impact. **(See Figure 52, page 70.)**

WEIGHT SHIFT

The correct use of your lower body to shift your weight toward the target helps minimize any excess up and down movement in your swing. Sliding your hips toward the target instead of turning them can cause your upper body to lean to the right. The low point of the swing moves to the right too, causing the club to bottom out and hit the ground before it reaches the ball.

❖ Turn your hips within the area of your stance on the downswing. Think of turning them between your feet. Avoid any sliding of your left hip toward the target; it should feel more like it's *turning* out of the way and moving back, behind you. Done properly, your left leg won't buckle out toward the target through impact. **(See Full Swing Basics, Figures 21A and 21B, page 37.)**

KNEES

Bend your knees too much during the downswing and the arc of your swing lowers, causing the club to bottom out behind the ball.

❖ Take practice swings without the ball. Concentrate on maintaining the same degree of flex in your knees throughout your swing. Stop and look at your knees to see if they have the same flex at these checkpoints: address, at the top of your backswing, and impact.

SHOTS TO THE LEFT
TO THE LEFT: *HOOKS*

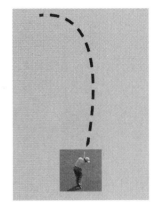

HOOK

Ball starts straight, then curves out of control to the left.

CLUBS
The factory may have produced a wood with a closed clubface angle, aiming the club to the left at address.

GRIP
A good swing causes your hands to return to the ball straight up and down, with the back of your left hand and the palm of your right pointing toward the target. With them in a strong position (turned clockwise) at address, at impact they will again be vertical—but now the clubface will be pointing to the left, causing the ball to hook. **(See Grip, pages 19-24.)**

❖ Avoid an overly strong grip. With a neutral or *slightly* strong grip, the back of your left hand and palm of the right should point at the target or just to the right and above it.

❖ Keep your grip pressure light in both hands. Right-hand grip pressure that is too tight accelerates the uncocking of your wrists—at impact the clubface points to the left prematurely, causing a hook. Keep your right-hand grip pressure equal to your left, and maintain that feeling all the way into the follow-through. Imagine holding an opened tube of toothpaste, or a stick of room temperature butter, or a live bird. Don't squeeze any of them.

ADDRESS
Hooking can start with a closed clubface at address, i.e., with the clubface pointing to the left of the target.
❖ Square the club by aligning the bottom leading edge perpendicular to the target line. **(See Aiming and Alignment, pages 27-28.)**

CASTING
Casting causes many things to happen too soon, including squaring up the clubface. The club ends up pointing to the left prematurely.
❖ **See Hinging and Unhinging of Wrists, pages 98-100; Casting, pages 45-47.**

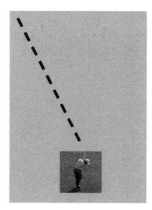

PULL

TO THE LEFT: PULLS

Ball starts and continues straight left.

SWING PATH
An outside-to-in swing path is the number one reason for pulls. The clubhead should approach the ball from inside the target line then travel down the line at impact, returning to the inside after striking the ball. When the club tracks toward the ball from outside the target line, a pull can result.
❖ **See Pull Slices, Swing Path, page 65.**

CLUBS
❖ The lie angle of your irons may be too upright. **(See Buying Clubs, page 165.)**

❖ The shafts of your irons may be too long. **(See Buying Clubs, page 165.)**

ADDRESS
Poor alignment can create an outside-to-in path relative to the target line, which causes pulls. **(See Aiming and Alignment, pages 27-28.)**
❖ Make sure your shoulders are square to the target line. Open shoulders (aimed to the left) cause your arms to swing out in that same direction, with the ball starting left. Take your address position and, while keeping your upper body as still as possible, slowly lift your club up and lay it horizontally across your shoulders. It should be parallel to the target line.

❖ Ironically, misalignment in the opposite direction can also cause pulls. When your body points directly at the target, a line parallel to your body and through the ball aims to the right of the target. This is actually a *closed* stance relative to your target line. Subconsciously, you'll *come over the top* in an attempt to pull the ball back on line. **(See Pushes, Address, page 68; Path, Outside-to-In, page 40.)**

BALL POSITION
Because of the correct inside-down-the-line-back-to-inside swing path, the ball can start left when played too far forward.
❖ Move the ball back in your stance, not more than a quarter of an inch at a time. Experiment with playing the ball somewhere between your left heel and the center of your stance.

DISCONNECTION

Arms *disconnected* from the bigger muscles of the shoulders are free to wander on the downswing **(See Connection, page 54)**, returning the clubhead to the ball on the wrong path—in this case outside-to-in at impact, causing a pulled shot.

❖ 'Plug' your left upper arm against your chest at your left armpit. Keep that area snug, but relaxed, throughout the backswing and until well after impact.

❖ Cultivate the one-piece takeaway. Move the triangle formed by your arms and shoulders in one piece during the swing, especially on the way back. Don't let your hands and arms control the backswing: it should feel as though your shoulders take your arms, hands, and the club back.

❖ Starting with the clubhead slightly off the ground at address can also promote a one-piece, connected takeaway.

PULL HOOK

TO THE LEFT: PULL HOOKS

Ball starts left, then curves even more in that direction.
❖ Review Pulls **(previous page)** and Hooks **(page 87)** individually for each component of this shot.

TO THE LEFT: SHANKS, WITH WOODS

These are shots that come off the rounded hosel where the shaft enters the clubhead. With the woods, shanks fly severely off line to the left.

ADDRESS

Standing too close to the ball establishes an erect spine with your arms hanging against your legs. Using your legs dynamically will cause your arms and the club to move out toward the ball to get past your driving lower body. The hosel lines up with the ball at impact, causing a shank.

❖ With your rear end sticking out behind you, tilt your spine forward so that your shoulders are out 1 to 4 inches past your toes at address; make sure your arms are relaxed and hanging like pieces of rope, straight down and well away from your legs. **(See Address, page 25.)**

SHANK/WOODS

CLUB POSITION
❖ Position the club's sweet spot, not the hosel, behind the ball at address.

HEAD AND SPINE MOVEMENT
Head movement, especially toward the target during the downswing, can cause shanking with the woods. Make sure your head stays behind the ball at impact.

❖ Imagine a metal pole running down your back and into the ground, keeping your spine in position at address and during the swing. **(Figure 51, page 70)** As your shoulders turn, your spine should stay against this pole—until well after impact.

❖ Keep your forehead lightly touching an imaginary wall, from address until your right shoulder comes into contact with your chin after impact. **(Figure 51, page 70)**

❖ Recreate and hold the perfect impact position for at least 30 seconds. Pay particular attention to keeping your upper body back behind the ball. This is a good drill to do in front of a mirror using **Figure 52, page 70** as your guide. Just a couple of minutes a day will increase your muscle memory for this position.

❖ Imagine a string attached from your right shoulder to the club shaft at the top of your backswing. **(See Figure 65, page 100.)** Keep the string attached during the downswing until your hands are near your right thigh. Do this drill with a steady spine and your head will stay behind the ball at impact.

BLADE OPEN AT IMPACT
The hosel can be the first part of the club to hit the ball when the clubface points severely to the right at impact.

❖ Ease the tension of your left hand on the grip: the club points to the right of the target at impact when your left hand grips the club too tightly. Try for light grip pressure with both hands from address to follow-through. Imagine holding an opened tube of toothpaste, or a stick of room temperature butter, or a live bird. Don't squeeze any of them. **(See Grip Pressure, page 21.)**

BLOCKING
You can *block* your way to a shank when your arms don't release. Blocking opens the clubface at impact, with the hosel leading the way into the ball. **(See Releasing, page 51.)** Try these three techniques to promote the correct release:

❖ Roll your forearms counterclockwise through impact from elbow to wrist. The clubface turns along with your forearms to square up when striking the ball. Stay relaxed to get the most from this drill.

❖ Try to touch your forearms together halfway into the follow-through when your right forearm is parallel to the ground. Bring your arms together near your wrists, not up by your elbows. **(Figure 45, page 64)**

❖ While keeping your left elbow close to your side, turn your left forearm counterclockwise in exactly the same way you would hit a left-handed, backhand, topspin shot while playing Ping-Pong. Keep your upper left arm against the left side of your chest through impact.

DISCONNECTION
When your arms disconnect from the bigger muscles of your shoulders, they are free to wander on the downswing. **(See Connection, page 54.)** This often returns the clubhead to the ball on the wrong path—either inside-to-out or outside-to-in, with the hosel hitting the ball. **(See Pull Slices, Swing Path, page 65.)**

❖ At address, 'plug' your left upper arm against your chest at your left armpit. Keep that area snug, but relaxed, throughout the backswing and until well after impact.

❖ Cultivate the one-piece takeaway. Move the triangle formed by your arms and shoulders in one piece during the swing, especially on the way back. Don't let your hands and arms control the backswing—it should feel as though your shoulders take your arms, hands, and the club back.

❖ Starting with the clubhead slightly off the ground at address can also promote a one-piece, connected takeaway.

SWING PATH
The wrong path can lead to a shank.

❖ Avoid laying the club off during the backswing. **(See Figure 25A, page 42.)** This can cause you to come *over the top*—where an overactive upper body causes the right shoulder to move out toward the ball, taking your hands and arms along and throwing the clubhead outside the target line.

❖ Initiate the downswing with your lower body to keep from coming over the top. Here are three ways to start the downswing properly: drive your right knee at the ball; turn your hips powerfully toward the target; drive your left knee at the target. But above all, the first move on the downswing must be with your lower body. **(See pages 36-38.)**

❖ As shown in **Figure 46, page 66**, put three golf balls down about two inches apart in a line set at a forty-five-degree angle to the target line. Practice hitting *only* the middle ball. To succeed, you are forced to swing the club from inside the target line as it approaches the ball, down the line at impact, and then back to the inside after the ball is struck. Because this drill can get three balls moving at once, use it only when the person in the stall immediately to your right is adequately protected.

❖ Keep the clubhead behind your body as long as possible on the downswing. **(See Figure 28, page 43.)**

❖ Hit the inside of the ball. Rather than the whole ball, aim to hit a specific area of it. **(Figure 47, page 67)**

❖ Casting can cause the clubhead to approach the ball on the wrong path (outside-to-in), leading to pulls. **(See Casting, bottom of page 85; and page 45.)**

❖ Take a cardboard box to the range. Lay it about an inch outside, and parallel to, the target line. As in **Figure 48, page 67**, line the ball up roughly in the middle of the side of the box. Try to hit the ball solidly without touching the box on either side of the ball. Don't pull away from the ball in an attempt to avoid the box.

❖ EXPERIMENT: Although the clubhead should travel back to the inside of the target line after impact, try to propel it out to the right of the target just after impact. Pick a landmark out on the horizon to the right of the target, and swing the clubhead out toward that object through impact. Often—even though it can feel excessive—exaggerating a move like this during the swing will just barely produce the correct position.

No Power

Everyone wants to hit the ball straight and far. The pros. You and I. Van Halen. The ex-Vice President. If you are making solid contact with the ball and hitting it fairly straight, but wish you could put more power behind your shots, this is the right chapter. Use these drills to repair any power leaks in your swing and refer to the pertinent pages in the Full Swing Basics chapter for a more detailed discussion of each power component.

BALANCE

To hit the ball solidly, stay well balanced in three key places in your swing: address, impact, and follow-through. By remaining in balance at the beginning and end of the swing, your chances of being balanced in the middle—at impact—skyrocket, as do your shots.

❖ With your back fairly straight, lean forward until your shoulders hang out between one and four inches past your toes. Stick your rear end out. Take your hands off the club and let your arms hang totally relaxed from your upper body. If they hang about a hand span away from your body, sixty percent of your weight is on the balls of your feet (with forty percent still on your heels), and your spine is correctly positioned, then you are balanced. **(See Address, pages 25-28.)**

❖ Take slow-motion practice swings without a ball, stopping at impact. Make sure you look like **Figure 52, page 70**: ninety percent of your weight on the left foot, right knee kicked in, right heel and outside edge of your right foot (even up by your little toe) off the ground, hips turned halfway or more to the target, straight line down the left shoulder through the hands to the ball, club shaft leaning slightly toward the target, right elbow tucked in close to the right side, and head behind the ball. Hold this position for at least five seconds to let muscle memory go to work. Every time you hold this perfect position you are rehearsing a balanced impact with the ball.

❖ Make a point of swinging your arms at the same rate on the downswing as they moved on the backswing. An unbalanced follow-through is often your body's way of saying you are trying to swing your arms too fast—at a pace your body can't handle. While the clubhead is coming through the ball at around 100 mph, during a good swing your arms will be moving much slower. **(See Clubhead Speed, pages 44-47.)**

❖ Fix your follow-through after every swing: belt buckle pointing at the target, ninety-five percent of your weight on your left foot, bottom of the right shoe pointing away from the target with no bend in the toes, spine erect, the club down your back—and hold this position for a count of five. Finishing in a controlled manner forces you to swing at a pace you can handle, resulting in a more balanced impact position. **(See Follow-Through, page 29.)**

❖ Make sure your left foot remains pointing toward 11:00 at the end of your swing. It's common for golfers to lose their balance in the follow-through because of the movement of their left foot: pivoting on the left heel as the ball of the left foot slides sideways, until their left shoe ends up pointing toward the target. This is like riding a surfboard or skateboard with your feet pointing in the same direction you're traveling—you won't be able to hold your equilibrium for long. Notice how people involved in board sports ride with their feet perpendicular to their line of travel. That's how they stay balanced.

BRACED RIGHT LEG

During the backswing, a quiet right leg combined with a complete shoulder turn supplies tremendous power. Keep your right leg still as your upper body coils fully against it—no hip or knee slide to the right. Learn also to shift seventy-five to eighty percent of your weight to the inside edge of your right foot on the way back. When your right hip, right knee, and weight slide to the outside of your right foot **(Figure 59, next page)** the coil is lost, and it's more difficult to shift your weight back toward the target. **(See The Role of the Right Leg, page 34.)**

❖ Take your address position with the outside edge of your right foot lifted just enough off the ground to fit a golf magazine underneath. Turning your shoulders fully, hit shots without letting that edge of your foot touch the ground during the backswing. Can you feel the coil? Keep in mind that this drill exaggerates the correct position; don't try to hold your foot away from the ground when playing on the course.

Figure 59

Figure 60

Morrie Kuhlmann

Morrie was losing consistency and power from his wandering right leg. His work has really paid off in relatively short time—he was in his 70th year before first picking up a club!

Age: 75

Playing Since: 1990

Time Spent on Project:
10 Weeks

Average Score: 87

Lowest Score: 81

Practice Schedule:
3 times per Week

Playing Schedule:
10 times per Month

Occupation:
Retired System Analyst

❖ Put a golf ball under the outside edge of your right foot at address. Like the previous drill, this helps to keep you loaded up on the inside of your right foot at the top of the backswing.

❖ Tape a string to your right knee. Knock your right knee in at address so that as you look down, the string hangs to the inside of your right foot. Stop at the top of your backswing and look at your knee—a braced right leg keeps the string hanging to the inside, or at worst, over the middle of your right foot. **(Figure 60, above; Coiling. . . , page 34)**

❖ Imagine building a hip-high brick wall next to your right leg. This wall leans in from bottom to top, mimicking the angle of your right leg at address. You are standing so close to it that your right leg rests against the bricks at address and during the backswing. The wall keeps your leg still and inhibits your hips from sliding to the right on the way back; while it does allow your hips to turn, it stops any lateral shift to the right. To ensure a proper weight shift, try to get your upper body out over the top of the wall slightly—enough that it would be possible to look down the outside of the wall and see the ground. **(Figure 60, insert)**

Ann Sparks

By reaching out for the ball, Ann was creating tension in her upper body before her swing even started. The effect was multiplied during the swing, robbing her shots of distance and accuracy.

Time Spent on Project:
3 Weeks

Average Score: 115

Practice Schedule:
2 to 3 times a Month

Playing Schedule:
Once a Month

Lowest Score: 109

Playing Since: 1994

Occupation:
Interior Designer

CLUBHEAD SPEED—RELAX

Clubhead speed starts with a relaxed upper body. Make sure to swing with a light grip and relaxed shoulders throughout. Your wrists should hinge and un-hinge freely. Remember, tight muscles travel much slower than relaxed muscles.

❖ Check your grip pressure at the end of your swing—it should be as light as it was at the beginning. **(See Grip Pressure, page 21.)**

❖ Relax your shoulders *completely* at address. Try to keep that feeling throughout the swing, and especially into the follow-through.

❖ After taking your address, open your left hand and let it hang, totally relaxed and straight down from your shoulder. If your hand falls closer to your body and not directly opposite the place on the grip where it would normally be, you're reaching for the ball and aren't relaxed enough. **(Figure 61, A and B)** Properly done, your left hand will hang opposite its position on the club. **(Figure 62, A and B)**

Figure 61   *Figure 62*

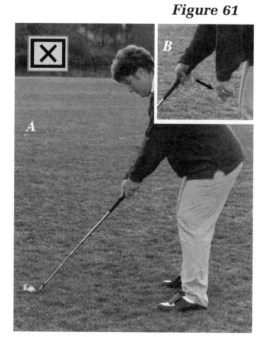

COILING—SHOULDERS

Turning your shoulders and winding your upper body fully against a braced right leg supplies power to your swing—you have to load the spring before unloading it. An incomplete shoulder turn can be one of the biggest power leaks in the golf swing. **(See The Role of the Right Leg, page 34.)**

The following backswing keys help take advantage of a full shoulder turn, and with it the coil:

❖ Turn your left shoulder until it is behind the ball.

❖ Cover your right foot with your left shoulder at the top of your backswing.

❖ Rotate your upper body until your back faces the target.

❖ Work on connection. **(See Connection, page 54.)**

❖ Keep in mind that without a braced right leg, none of the points above matter. **(See Braced Right Leg, page 94; The Role of the Right Leg, page 34.)**

DIVOTS

Hitting down, compressing the ball between the clubface and ground increases the length of your shots considerably. This downward motion of the clubhead produces divots to the left of the ball. **(See Divots, page 56.)** With the following drills, picture the clubface pointing down at the ground at impact—not up at the sky. Even though this is an exaggeration of where the clubface really is at impact, thinking in this way often creates the correct position. Remember, *hitting down* does not mean swinging harder or faster. It means changing the angle the clubhead travels on as it approaches the ball.

❖ Pinch, trap, or compress the ball between the clubface and the ground at impact. Nick Faldo calls it *squeezing* the ball away. Picture the club leaning toward the target with a straight line down the left arm, wrist, and club shaft. **(See Figure 52, page 70.)**

❖ Drive the ball down into a spot on the ground about half an inch to the left of the ball. **(See Figure 57, page 79.)**

❖ Before each shot at the range, turn the ball so the brand name or range stripe is at the top back quarter. Make the clubface come into the ball at that angle to get the sweet spot striking the stripe or brand name. **(See Figure 58, page 79.)**

❖ Without a ball, take practice swings with the club moving down, contacting the ground after it passes the ball's usual place in your stance. In other words, try to take a shallow divot in front (on the target side) of the imaginary ball.

❖ Push a tee into the ground about an inch in front of your ball; leave a quarter of an inch of the tee sticking out of the ground. Hit the tee after striking the ball to learn to hit down. When hitting off a mat, focus on a spot a half inch in front of the ball; make sure your club strikes the mat there.

FULL FOLLOW-THROUGH

Ensure an accelerating clubhead by swinging beyond impact to a full follow-through. **(See Follow-Through, page 29. Note the club's position.)**
❖ Put yourself into the complete follow-through position after every swing: ninety-five percent of your weight on your left foot, belt buckle pointing at the target, bottom of the right shoe pointing away from the target with no bend in the toes of your right foot, spine erect, and the club all the way down your back. Hold this completely balanced position for a count of five.

HINGING AND UNHINGING OF WRISTS

The natural, unforced cocking and uncocking of your wrists supplies clubhead speed. **(See Clubhead Speed, page 44.)** Your wrists hinge on the backswing due to the momentum and weight of the clubhead—without any effort on your part. Likewise, they should unhinge through impact because of centrifugal force, not from your labor. Most amateur golfers unhinge their wrists prematurely on the downswing in a rush to hit the ball. **(Figure 63, next page)** This is called *casting*—because it's the same motion used when casting out the line from a fishing pole. **(See Casting, page 45.)**

WARNING! Some of the following drills are an exaggerated version of the actual move. Often it's beneficial to try to overdo a movement in the golf swing: usually, you'll just barely reach the correct position. Study the appropriate Figures throughout this book to compare the correct positions to the overstated positions of these drills.

❖ Try to get your hands to pass the ball before the clubhead reaches it. Feel as though the clubhead is lagging a couple of feet behind your hands through impact. **(Figure 64, below)**

❖ With your wrists fully hinged at the top of your backswing, imagine a string attached from the club shaft to your right shoulder. **(Figure 65, next page)** On the downswing, try to keep this string fastened to your shoulder until your hands reach a point opposite your right thigh. This maintains the hinge of your wrists longer through the ball.

Rick Torseth

Probably the most difficult problem to fix in the swing, Rick has been working on a *late hit* for almost 6 months. Gradually he has seen longer, straighter shots.

Time Spent on Project:
22 Weeks

Average Score: 97

Practice Schedule:
Once a Week

Playing Schedule:
Once a Week

Lowest Score: 93

Playing Since: 1970

Occupation:
Consultant

Figure 63

Figure 64

Figure 65:
String attached to club; right elbow peeking out.

Figure 66:
Angle at back of right hand.

❖   Think of your right elbow leading your hands down from the top of your backswing. Imagine your elbow getting to the ball first as your hands and the clubhead lag behind. Conversely, when your right elbow stops moving on the downswing, you'll immediately start to cast. Here's another way to think of this drill: a person looking directly at you should see your right elbow peeking out below your left arm during much of the downswing. **(Figure 65, to the left)**

❖   Stop at the top of your backswing. Imagine your shoulders, arms, and hands are one solid, connected unit. Without using your arms and shoulders to pull the club down, *slowly* turn your hips and push off your right foot, shifting your weight into the follow-through. Feel your upper body being pulled down—solely from the action of your lower body—as your wrists stay cocked. To get the most from this drill, keep your spine at a constant angle. Practice these slow-motion swings without a ball at first. Then try it with a golf ball. Take the same unhurried swing without any thoughts about distance or direction; just try to get a sense of your uncoiling lower body doing the work.

❖   Learn to take divots. With the club shaft leaning to the left, imagine the clubface pointing down as it strikes the ball. **(See Divots, page 56.)**

❖   Ala Nick Faldo, keep the back of your right hand as close as you can to your right forearm, on the downswing and through impact. **(Figure 66, to the left)**

❖   Assume the correct impact position with the clubhead placed behind something solid on the ground, like a door jamb or bench leg. Make sure you look *exactly* like **Figure 52, page 70**: ninety percent of your weight on the left foot, right knee kicked in, right heel and outside edge of your right foot (even up by your little toe) off the ground, hips turned halfway or more to the target, straight line down the left shoulder through the hands to the ball, club shaft leaning slightly toward the target, right elbow tucked in close to the right side, and head behind the ball. Now for the anti-casting move: pressing the first knuckle of your right index finger against the grip, bow the shaft of the club slightly out to the left and hold this position for at least 15 to 30 seconds. Try to keep that pressure in the shaft during the downswing and you will learn to lead into impact with your hands, not the clubhead.

INSIDE PATH OF CLUBHEAD

Your club should approach the ball from inside the target line to insure solid contact on the sweet spot and to hit the ball where you are aiming. Refer to **Swing Path, page 39** for a detailed description of the correct path.

❖ Imagine the wagon wheel described in **The Spine, page 33**. Take slow-motion swings without a ball, guiding the clubhead along the rim of that wheel. Try to hit balls with that same swing, first at slower, then at regular speed.

❖ **See Pull Slices, Swing Path, page 65**.

❖ **See Swing Plane "...and on the way down," page 43.**

❖ **See both drills starting on page 37 of Leg Drive.**

❖ Your right elbow should pass close to your right hip on the way to impact. **(See Swing Path, pages 39-40.)**

LEG DRIVE

Put more emphasis on starting the downswing with your lower body. **(See page 36.)** Try each of these triggers for your first move down from the top of your backswing:

❖ Kick your right knee in at the ball.

❖ Turn and clear your hips—specifically your left hip turning behind you— powerfully toward the target.

❖ Plant your left heel while driving the weight off the inside edge of your right foot.

❖ Drive your left knee toward the target.

❖ **See both drills starting on page 37 of Leg Drive.**

RELEASING

A full release **(Releasing, Page 51)** of the arms through impact has the same powerful effect on the ball as a topspin shot in tennis: it creates a lower, more penetrating trajectory through the air, and by causing the ball to roll forward once it hits the ground, the release can greatly increase the overall distance of your tee shots.

❖ Roll your forearms counterclockwise through impact from elbow to wrist. The clubface turns along with your forearms to square up when striking the ball. Stay relaxed to get the most from this drill.

❖ Try to touch your forearms together halfway into the follow-through, when your right forearm is parallel to the ground. Bring your arms together near your wrists, not up by your elbows. **(Figure 45, page 64)**

❖ While keeping your left elbow close to your side, turn your left forearm counterclockwise in exactly the same way you would hit a left-handed, backhand, topspin shot while playing Ping-Pong. Keep your upper left arm against the left side of your chest through impact.

SWEET SPOT

Powerful shots depend on striking the ball with the sweet spot of your club. Off-center hits transfer less energy to the ball, resulting in a loss of distance. Exactly where the sweet spot is on your irons depends on their design, but it should be near the middle of the clubface. It will be in the middle with your woods.

ADDRESS
❖ Position the sweet spot of the clubface directly behind the ball to start with. That's where it should return at impact.

❖ Let your arms hang straight down at address. Don't reach for the ball! Your arms will come back too close to your body, pulling the clubhead with them. You'll hit the ball off the toe of the club, most likely causing a weak slice.

HEAD AND SPINE MOVEMENT

Keep your head and spine steady throughout the swing. **(See The Spine, page 33.)** Any extra movement makes it very difficult to get the sweet spot on the ball.

❖ Imagine a metal pole running down your back and into the ground, keeping your spine in position at address and during the swing. **(Figure 51, page 70)** As your shoulders turn, your spine should stay against this pole—until well after impact.

❖ Keep your forehead lightly touching an imaginary wall, from address until your right shoulder comes into contact with your chin after impact. **(Figure 51, page 70)**

❖ Recreate and hold the perfect impact position for at least 30 seconds. Pay particular attention to keeping your upper body back behind the ball. This is a good drill to do in front of a mirror using **Figure 52, page 70** as your guide. A couple of minutes a day increases your muscle memory for this position.

❖ Imagine a string attached from your right shoulder to the club shaft at the top of your backswing. **(See Figure 65, page 100.)** Try to keep the string attached during the downswing, until your hands are near your right thigh. Do this drill with a steady spine and your head will stay behind the ball at impact.

DISCONNECTION

Disconnected from the bigger muscles of your shoulders, your arms are free to wander on the downswing. **(See Connection, pages 54-55.)** This often returns the clubhead to the ball on the wrong path, missing the sweet spot and causing a weak shot.

❖ 'Plug' your left upper arm against your chest at your left armpit. Keep that area snug, but relaxed, throughout the backswing and until well after impact.

❖ Cultivate the one-piece takeaway. Move the triangle formed by your arms and shoulders in one piece during the swing, especially on the way back. Don't let your hands and arms control the backswing—it should feel as though your shoulders take your arms, hands, and the club back.

❖ Starting with the clubhead slightly off the ground at address can also promote a one-piece, connected takeaway.

TEMPO/RHYTHM

Tempo is the overall speed of the swing, while rhythm is the speed of the back-swing compared to that of the downswing. Many of the best golfers swing slowly—just watch Nancy Lopez or Payne Stewart. Others have faster swings—like Nick Price or Jose Marie Olazabal. Generally it takes a person with excellent mechanics and eye-hand coordination to swing quickly; the rest of us will find great benefit in taking slower swings. While no single tempo is perfect for all of us, there is an appropriate tempo for *each* of us.

❖ Make your backswing and downswing evenly paced for better rhythm. Take practice swings concentrating on your arms coming down at the same speed they went back and up.

❖ Stay *completely* relaxed with your upper body throughout the swing. Keeping all tension out of your shoulders, arms, and hands makes it very difficult to swing out of control.

UPPER BODY BACK AT IMPACT

Pushes, shanks, skyed drives, and a general loss of power are all possible when your head gets in front of the ball.

❖ Keep your upper body completely relaxed and passive while driving your lower body powerfully during the downswing. **(See Leg Drive, page 36.)**

❖ To turn your shoulders around the fixed axis of your spine, keep your forehead lightly touching an imaginary wall, from address until well after impact. Keep it there until your right shoulder comes into contact with your chin. **(See Figure 51, page 70.)**

❖ Recreate and hold the perfect impact position for 15 to 30 seconds, paying particular attention to your upper body hanging back behind the ball. Make sure the left side of your head is to the right of the ball. This is a good drill to do in front of a mirror using **Figure 52, on page 70** as your guide—a couple of minutes a day will help ingrain the muscle memory.

❖ Imagine a string attached from your right shoulder to the club shaft at the top of your backswing. **(See Figure 65, page 100.)** Keep the string attached on the downswing until your hands are near your right thigh. Do this drill with a steady spine and your head should stay behind the ball at impact.

❖ Here's one Seve Ballesteros worked on as a youth: Try to move your head slightly (one to three inches) to the *right* while swinging down through impact. It may feel as though your head moves three feet when it's really only moving a couple of inches; have a friend tell you exactly how much movement there is. But watch out! This drill makes it more difficult to shift your weight properly toward the target because much of your weight will hang back to the right along with your head.

WEIGHT SHIFT

Just as in throwing a football or baseball—or for that matter, almost any other sport that involves moving something in your hands—the more aggressive the weight shift, the more power is generated. **(See Weight Shift, page 31.)**

WEIGHT SHIFT—BACKSWING
Notice, when shifting your weight properly to the right against a braced right leg, how your back angles away from the target while your right leg leans in the other direction, toward the target. **(See Figure 20, page 35.)** Avoid a reverse pivot—your back leaning to the left with most of your weight planted on your left foot. **(Figure 67, next page.)**
❖ Consciously move your head to the right during the first three feet of your backswing. Between one-fourth inch to three or four inches will be enough to get your upper body behind the ball and your weight shifted.

❖ Use this drill with or without a club: stand in front of a mirror and take your backswing, stopping at the top. Check your position for the angle of your back and a complete weight shift. (Compare to **Figure 20, page 35.**) Make any necessary corrections, then hold this position for fifteen seconds.

❖ Make sure your left shoulder is behind the ball at the top of your backswing.

Aldie Amundson

Aldie's concern over a general lack of distance lead her to work on a better weight shift. In relatively short order she tamed her reverse weight shift, learning to load more weight on her right side at the top of her backswing.

Time Spent on Project:
3 Weeks

Average Score: 94

Practice Schedule:
2 to 3 times a Week

Playing Schedule:
Once a Week

Lowest Score: 90

Playing Since: 1970

Occupation:
Retired

Figure 67

Figure 68

❖ Cover your right foot with your left shoulder at the top of your backswing.

❖ Imagine a line coming straight up from the ball. Without sliding your hips to the right, turn and shift your weight so most of your body is to the right side of the line. **(Figure 68, above)**

Weight shift—Downswing

❖ Stop at the top of your backswing. Think of everything in your upper body (hands, arms, and shoulders) as one solid, connected unit. Without using your arms and shoulders, *slowly* uncoil your hips and push off your right foot, shifting your weight and turning into the follow-through. Feel your upper body being pulled down solely from the action of your lower body—especially as your hips turn to face the target. Keep your spine at a constant angle. This drill will improve your swing in three ways: (1) you'll learn to start the downswing with your legs and hips, not your upper body; (2) using your lower body to initiate the downswing helps to ensure the proper inside path for the club to approach the ball on; (3) your wrists will remain hinged longer into the impact area, generating more clubhead speed (the late hit).

MISSING THE BALL

Whiffs—we hate 'em. They're embarrassing and they cost us a stroke. Everyone at one time or another has had to endure completely missing the ball, especially when first taking up golf.

ADDRESS

You're standing too close at address and swinging the club around to the outside of the ball. Or you're standing too far away, causing the clubhead to swing between yourself and the ball.

❖ Nail down your address position. Make sure your shoulders are hanging out between one and four inches past your toes. Your arms should hang straight down with about a hand-span of space between your legs and hands. Don't reach for the ball. Here's a good test: from your normal address position, let go of the club with your left hand and let your left arm hang totally relaxed. If it hangs next to the place it would be on the club, you're all set. Otherwise, when your left arm swings closer to your body, you're standing too far away and reaching for the ball. **(See Figure 61, page 96.)**

BALL POSITION

The swing is shaped like a big circle, and where the circle touches the ground is where the clubhead strikes the ball. This low point for the swing is slightly to the left of the base of your neck. With the ball positioned too far to the left of this low point the club will be moving up, missing the ball completely.

❖ Take some practice swings and note where the club makes its most consistent contact with the grass or mat. Play the ball about a quarter of an inch to the right of that spot to make solid contact with the ball first, then the ground. **(See Divots, page 56.)**

PRACTICE SWINGS

❖ Take practice swings with your clubhead touching the ground. Practice this at home (use an old carpet or welcome mat) or at the range, but don't swing at any object—no whiffle ball, leaf, cigarette butt, or anything else. Make sure the club *touches* the ground or mat exactly where the ball would be in your stance. As you improve, learn to hit a spot just to the left of the ball. **(See Divots, page 56.)**

WEIGHT DISTRIBUTION AT IMPACT

Most of your weight (eighty to ninety percent) should be on your left foot at impact. With it loaded up on your right foot instead, your head and spine hang back too far, moving the low point of the swing behind the ball. The clubhead moves up through impact, passing right over the top of the ball.

❖ To shift your weight on the downswing:
   1. Kick your right knee in at the ball.
   2. Turn and clear your hips—specifically your left hip turning behind you—powerfully toward the target.
   3. Plant your left heel while driving the weight off the inside edge of your right foot.
   4. Drive your left knee toward the target.

❖ **See both drills starting on page 37 of Leg Drive.**

❖ Make sure no more than fifty-five percent of your weight is on your right foot at address. Otherwise it's likely your weight will stay there as you strike the ball.

HEAD AND SPINE MOVEMENT

Lifting your head and spine up at any time between address to just after impact pulls the club up off the ground. The top of a ball is only 1.68 inches off the ground. A spine that moves up two or three inches on the backswing causes the club to pull up the same distance. You'll completely miss the ball unless there is some sort of compensating downward move on the way to impact.

❖ **See Head and Spine Movement, page 69.**

POPPED-UP TEE SHOTS

You've teed up your ball, it goes straight up in the air, and now you're teed off. A skyed shot with your woods occurs when the top of the club hits the bottom of the ball. Check these fundamentals to solve the problem.

BALL POSITION
Playing the ball too far back in the stance creates a downward blow at impact. The top of the club catches the bottom of the ball, sending it skyward.

❖ Check your ball position using a couple of clubs. Place one parallel to the target line across your toes, grip end toward the target. Put a second club between your feet and perpendicular to the target line, crossing the clubs at the base of the grips. Play the ball about six inches off the grip end of the second club. Your left heel should be right next to that second club, or up to three or four inches to the left of it. **(Figure 69, below)**

Figure 69:
Criss-cross clubs to check for ball position.

❖ When measuring to the ball, stand with your feet together, with the ball off your left heel. Widen your stance by moving your right foot—make only minor adjustments with your left. This keeps the ball forward in your stance. Work this into your pre-shot routine. **(See Pre-Shot Routine, page 57.)**

❖ EXPERIMENT: Try playing the ball between one and four inches to the right of your left heel.

TEEING THE BALL TOO HIGH

With too much space between the ball and the ground, the club will easily pass underneath the ball. At address, the rule of thumb is to tee the ball up so that the top of the wood is about even with the equator of the ball.

❖ Take your address position. After setting the club down, hold the shaft very steady and step back behind the ball, looking down the target line. If too much of the ball is above the top of the clubhead, adjust the height of the tee.

HEAD MOVES FORWARD

Is your tee flattened and pushed into the divot's hole at the end of the swing? When your head moves forward during the downswing, your upper body and the club follow: the club reaches the bottom part of its arc after striking the ball. Remember, when hitting teed shots with a wood, the club should be moving level or slightly upward when striking the ball.

❖ Keep your left cheek (the one on your face) to the right of the ball at impact.

WOUNDED DUCKS

These are teed-up *iron shots* that get off the ground and go fairly straight, but they don't sound or feel good, lack velocity coming off the clubface, and fall short of their normal distance. You are catching the ball with the top grooves of your irons, missing the sweet spot by about an inch *too high* on the clubface. Usually only the following produces these shots with teed-up irons:

❖ The tee is too high. Try to recreate a perfect lie from the fairway when teeing your irons up, with the top of the tee no more than a quarter of an inch above the ground. In other words, the ball should be sitting just above the ground. Strive to take a divot like any other normal iron shot. **(See Divots, page 56.)**

CHAPTER FOUR

SHORT GAME BASICS

The short game—putting, chipping, pitching, and bunker shots—is the key to shooting lower scores. It's possible to work on your full swing for a whole year and see your average score go down by only five strokes. But practice your short game diligently for two months and you can lower your handicap ten strokes or more.

Two features of golf-course design best emphasize the importance of the short game:

1. THE GREENS—PAR

Every green is designed to be *two*-putted. On a par three, for example, you are meant to reach the green with your first shot, then take two putts; par fours should be reached in two shots, then two-putted; and you have three shots to reach the par fives, then two putts. Getting your ball onto the green in the prescribed number of strokes is called reaching the green *in regulation*—TV broadcasters often refer to "greens in regulation" when discussing a touring pro's expertise.

Even for the pros, consistently hitting the greens is a tough assignment. When watching the tour players on TV, you may think they reach all the greens in regulation every round they play. However, the broadcasts only show the last groups, the players who are beating the rest of the field. You are viewing the best players on tour—at that moment. The very next week, some of those same golfers won't get

any TV time because they'll be having a tough time hitting the broadside of a cart barn. Remarkably, at year's end the tour leaders in the "Greens in Regulation" category hit only eleven or twelve greens in a typical round. Averaged out over the year, the best of the best still miss *one third* of the greens in regulation.

Yet they still shoot par or better. Why? Because they can compensate for a poor full shot with their short game finesse: chipping, pitching, and putting.

Let's look at the impact that just putting can have on your scores. Imagine having played a perfect round of golf on your favorite course: you hit all the greens in regulation, and took exactly two putts to put the ball into each cup. Two putts per hole, over 18 holes, equals 36 putts. On a par 72 course, shooting even par 72 with exactly 36 putts, means your putting equaled fifty percent of your score.

Think about that for a moment—you just hit your full shots perfectly, *yet putting still accounted for one half of all your strokes.*

The conclusion: working just on your putting can improve half your score, especially during those not-so-perfect rounds.

The second element of golf course design that makes the short game so important is:

2. THE LENGTH OF THE HOLES

Naturally our chances of reaching the green in regulation decrease as the holes get longer. Under the USGA guidelines (see below), playing par threes at the extreme distances of 250 yards for men and 210 yards for women, we stand a good chance of missing the green on our first shot. To make par when we do miss, we'll have to put our second shot close to the cup, then sink the first putt.

That same plan applies to the 400- to 470-yard par fours and 575-yard par fives. Factor in wet grass and the wind in your face, and some holes will play even longer. The bottom line: even when we are playing our best, most golf courses have at least a few long and difficult holes that we can't reach in regulation—these monster holes demand a solid short game.

Yardage Guidelines

From the *USGA Rules of Golf*, here are the general yardage guidelines for determining par:

PAR	MEN	WOMEN
3	up to 250 yards	up to 210 yards
4	251 to 470	211 to 400
5	471 and over	401 to 575
6		576 and over

PUTTING

There isn't just one way to putt. But if you are unhappy with your putting stroke, there is a certain degree of safety in copying the methods used by the majority of touring professionals. The information that follows includes these methods; use them as a starting point in the search for your own personal putting style.

Almost everything about the putting stroke is optional. Sam Snead putts side-saddle, with both feet on the left side of the target line. Jack Nicklaus bends considerably from the waist at address, while Don January stands almost totally erect. Peter Senior, from the European Tour, rests the putter grip against his chin. And look at the long putters used by many of the players on the Seniors' tour.

GRIP

Many grips can work, but you would do well to copy the grip used by at least seventy percent of the pros—the reverse-overlap. Take your normal grip, the one you use with your irons and woods, then remove your right hand from the club. While still holding the club with your thumb and the last three fingers of your left hand, point your left index finger away from the shaft. **(Figure 70)** Put your right hand back on the club three inches above your left, and wrap all the fingers of your right hand around the club. Now slide your right hand down toward your left (with your left index finger still off the shaft), until your right little finger comes to rest

Figure 70

against the middle finger of your left hand. Your left index finger should be on the outside of the last one, two, or three fingers of your right hand, depending on what feels most comfortable. **(Figure 71)** At this point the club should also be more in your palms, not your fingers.

The reverse-overlap grip benefits your putting stroke in two ways. First, it enhances eye-hand coordination, because all the fingers of the right hand, including the little finger, are now on the club. Being completely on the grip, your dominant right hand— the hand used for most everyday tasks—yields better touch and control. Second, the overlapping left index finger inhibits wrist action. With your

Figure 71:
Reverse-overlap
putting grip.

wrists out of the picture there are fewer moving parts and that means a more repeatable stroke.

Give this grip a fair trial—I have many students who find the reverse overlapping grip uncomfortable at first, but within thirty minutes they are hooked.

Other grip options to try:

Cross-handed—the left and right hands switch places. This puts your left hand in the dominant position so your left wrist is less likely to break down through impact. **(Figure 72A)** Watch Fred Couples and Tom Kite.

Palms turned toward the sky, instead of facing each other. This also helps immobilize your wrists through the stroke. **(Figure 72B)**

You can try Bernard Langer's grip. I'm not sure if it has a name, but with your right hand holding the top of the shaft against your left forearm, it should inhibit any movement from your left wrist. **(Figure 72C)**

Overlapping or interlocking—the same grip you use with your woods and irons. **(See page 20.)**

GRIP PRESSURE

Unlike the full swing, where you need very relaxed hands, putting grip pressure can be light, firm, or somewhere in between. Experiment until you find the grip pressure that is light enough to feel the clubhead, but firm enough to keep it from wobbling off line.

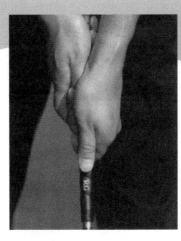

Figure 72A:
Cross-Handed

PUTTING GRIPS

Figure: 72B:
Opposing Palms

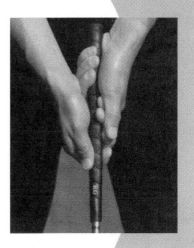

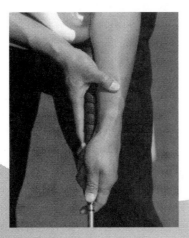

Figure 72C:
The Langer Grip

Start with your feet shoulder-width apart; experiment with a slightly narrower or wider stance, but avoid the extremes. Point both feet straight up to 12 o'clock so each foot is at right angles to the target line. A line across your toes should be parallel to the target line. **(Figure 73)**

Experiment with the following options until you find the address that's right for you:

1. Open your stance, with the left foot pulled slightly back from the line. (Your shoulders remain square.) It may be easier to follow through out to the hole with your lower body open to the target line. **(Figure 74)**

2. Set your right foot at 12 o'clock and your left foot at 11 o'clock, just like the full swing address. This should be a familiar position.

3. Try both feet toed in slightly, pigeon style—this can create a tripod effect for better balance. Watch Arnold Palmer.

Now, flex your knees slightly and bend forward from the waist, until your eyes are either directly over the ball, or just inside the target line (between your feet and the ball). **(See Figure 73.)** This brings your eyes closer to the ball, improving eye-hand coordination, and helps you see the line of the putt. Put the sweet spot of the putter directly behind the ball at address. For more on locating the sweet spot, **see page 141.**

Figure 73

Figure 74

ADDRESS

A stable, quiet, comfortable putting position is essential. The more at ease you are with your address position, the more time you will spend on the practice greens hitting putts.

Arms and Elbows

Options also exist for your arms and elbows: At address you could have your:

1. Arms hanging away from your body. **(Figure 75A)**
2. Elbows close to your sides. **(Figure 75B)**
3. Elbows bent. **(Figure 75C)**
4. Arms straight. **(Figure 75D)**

Whichever arm position you choose, try to set an imaginary line across the top of your forearms parallel to the target line. **(Figure 76, below)**

Figure 75A:
Arms out.

Figure 75B:
Elbows in.

Figure 75C:
Elbows bent.

Figure 76

Figure 75D:
Arms straight.

Ball Position

Proper positioning of the ball at address promotes many things, including a smooth-rolling putt. If the ball bounces along the green instead of rolling, moving the ball an inch or two forward or back in your stance can help solve the problem. Find the position that creates the smoothest roll: start with the ball in the middle of your stance and gradually move it forward until it is opposite your left big toe; the correct ball position for you will probably be somewhere in that range.

Weight Distribution

Here are two good options: (1) distribute your weight evenly between your feet, or (2) lean slightly toward the target, with sixty percent of your weight on your left foot. Study Greg Norman's putting address to see this clearly. Leaning the shaft of the putter toward the target also helps get your weight to the left at address and yields more solid putts.

The Stroke

The putting stroke is often compared to a pendulum, with the club moving smoothly back and through. As you hold your putter at address, notice the triangle formed by your shoulders and arms. Your shoulders are the base of this triangle and your arms make up the sides. **(Figure 77)** Move only this triangle when you swing your putter: getting a big part of your body, your shoulders, in control of this pendulum means more consistent putting. The hole is only 4.25 inches in diameter, and the slightest bit of movement with the rest of your body—head, spine, legs—can send the ball off line, missing the cup.

Put a premium on keeping your head perfectly still—this is one ingredient that *all* good putters work on. Many of them don't look up until they hear the ball dropping in the cup, or at least until it has had time to reach the hole. They want to be looking down at the empty spot on the green where the ball used to be.

Figure 77

The size of your backswing determines how far the ball travels; keep it small for a shorter putt, and longer to cover a greater distance.

Your follow-through helps determine the line the putt travels on. Try to feel as though you are pushing the ball out toward the hole. Don't stop your follow-through at the ball—you won't know for sure which direction your putter head is traveling. Keep your clubhead moving out toward the cup through impact and the ball will go in that direction.

These two stroke options are common on tour:
1. "Popping" the ball with a short backswing and a slightly longer follow-through. This kind of stroke works well on bumpy, less manicured greens, i.e., most public courses. Watch Paul Azinger to see this stroke in action.
2. A flowing stroke, with a bigger backswing and follow-through, out toward the hole. Use this stroke on fast, smooth greens, the kind found on courses with less play—for example, resort courses and most country clubs. Try to keep your tempo slow and smooth. Ben Crenshaw is the model here.

Reading the Greens

Reading the break correctly takes you halfway to a successful putt. As if there aren't enough problems getting to the green, once there, you'll find the golf course architects have built in all kinds of ridges, knolls, and valleys under the putting surface to make things more challenging. These hills greatly affect the direction your putts take. It's no coincidence that the best putters in the world are also the best at reading the break—figuring out exactly what those mounds are going to do to their putts.

To read the break accurately, squat down close to the ground to get a better look at the terrain. Johnny Miller, one of the best players in the world in the 1970's, once suggested a great way to judge the slopes: imagine pouring a big vat of chocolate milk all over the target line between your ball and the hole. Where do you "see" the milk puddles collecting? If, for example, most of the milk gathers near your ball, you will be heading uphill. If the milk ends up to the left of the target line, the green breaks that way and your ball will curve in that direction on the way to the hole. Even though I use this method on medium to long putts, it's invaluable on those short four- to six-foot putts, especially the ones that look straight in. Pouring milk on the target line to double-check my read, I often see some break I hadn't noticed at first.

Now refine the general impression obtained from the spilled milk by determining the exact line for your putt to travel on into the cup. Here are two popular, but very different, methods:

❖ Think of hitting a *straight* putt to an imaginary target. For example, if you think your ball will break twelve inches to the right of the hole, try to hit a straight putt at an imaginary hole twelve inches to the *left* of the real cup. **(Figure 78)**

❖ Visualize the *curving* line of your upcoming putt on the green. Picture that line vividly—on fire, or painted fluorescent orange—anything to get it firmly in your mind. Try to roll the ball directly over that line, and into the hole. **(Figure 79)**

Whichever way works best, consider this: the best putters in the world often say they won't step up to putt the ball until they first "see" (with their mind's eye) the ball rolling along the correct line and into the cup. This will help you precisely define the line, and because you are programming a positive result—the ball falling to the bottom of the cup—your confidence will soar.

Along with the perfect line, the perfect putt needs to be hit with perfect *speed*. And that makes the other half of a successful putt, judging the speed of the greens, just as important as reading the break accurately.

Fast greens allow the ball to curve more than slower greens, and both make reading the break a more

Figure 78:
Putting to an
imaginary hole.

Figure 79:
Visualize a curving
putt to hole.

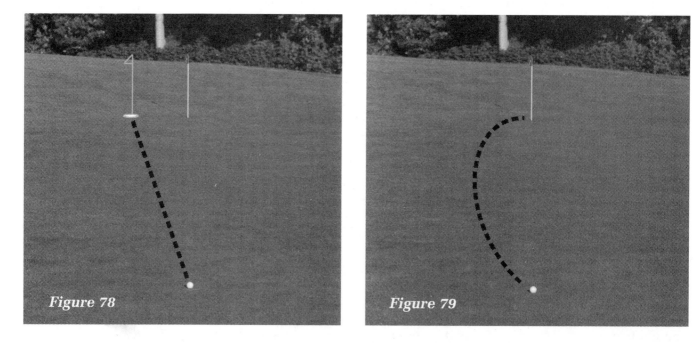

Figure 78

Figure 79

complicated matter. For example, if you determine the correct line on a fast green, but misjudge the speed and hit the ball too softly, the ball won't hold the line. As it slows down coming up short, it also curves off to the side. In the same situation, with a putt hit too hard, the ball travels straight past the hole without taking the break.

At least three factors having to do with the greens themselves can affect the speed of your putt: (1) wet greens are slower than dry greens; (2) uncut greens are slower than those that have been recently mowed; (3) hills—uphill putts move much slower than downhill putts. One of the best ways to improve your ability to judge the speed of greens is to practice on the varying terrain of different greens. As they say, there is no substitute for experience.

Before every round of golf give yourself 15 to 30 minutes to spend on the course's practice putting green. Theoretically, all the greens on the course will be set up and maintained like that green—recently mowed or watered, flat or hilly, etc.

One other thing—it is in your interest to help keep the practice greens of the world in as good a shape as possible. Be especially careful not to drag your golf shoes or clubs across them. And after you have hit your putts, chips, or pitches, don't knock the balls back off the green with the clubhead. Gently collect them into a pile and put them back in the basket by hand.

PUTTING STRATEGIES

Walk The Putt

One of the first things you should do after reaching the green is to walk the length of your putt. This gives you an idea of how much break you have to negotiate and supplies accurate feedback about the distance your ball has to cover. Your feet will also relay information about the condition of the green—the severity of the slope, whether it's wet, etc.

A Bigger Target

Surprisingly, many pros are not aiming for the cup on longer putts, but rather a larger area around the hole. For example, when they are fifteen feet away they might think of putting the ball into a circle having a six-inch radius. Their strategy is two-fold: (1) if they miss and leave the ball inside the circle, their second putt will be a no-brainer and, (2) there is less pressure aiming at a bigger target; they are more likely to take a smooth stroke.

This method contributes to fewer three-putt greens. Start by trying to leave your first putt in an area around the cup within the radius of a putter shaft; on longer putts of 30 feet or more, use a larger circle, say, with a six foot radius. Make the circles smaller as you become more proficient.

Downhill Putts

You have two choices when facing a downhill putt. Both have risks—the stroke you choose has everything to do with your temperament and the speed of the greens:

1. The Dribble—barely touch the ball and watch it lazily work its way down to the cup. The putting surface needs to be smooth and fast to have the best chance of sinking this kind of putt; avoid this one if the greens maintenance crew has been recently laid off—the ball won't hold its line as it slowly coasts down the hill. It becomes susceptible to every jagged blade and bump of grass in its path, slithering down the slope like a meandering snake. You won't know the outcome of your stroke until the last split second—with the ball either miraculously falling into the cup, or more likely, watching it head glacier-like toward the middle of the hole, only to veer off line at the last possible moment.

2. The Slam Dunk—use a firm stroke to boldly send the ball down the hill and into the back of the hole, where it drops to the bottom of the cup. This is the stroke to consider when faced with beat-up greens. The percentages are with you when ramming the ball through the irregular surface of a poorly mowed green. The down side to this strategy is if you miss it, you will miss it *big*. While your first putt might be a five footer, your second could be from twenty feet beyond the cup—coming back up the hill.

Also try this slam-dunking approach to tame a short, breaking putt when you are on a smooth, fast green. If you coast the ball in, it might curve eight inches or more on the way to the hole. But by using a firmer stroke you can play for half that amount of break, making it an easier putt to judge. Again, watch out if you miss the hole.

Uphill Putts

It's worth repeating the old joke that ninety percent of all putts that come up short of the hole never go in. You have to get the ball there to give it any chance of dropping. When putting uphill you should have less fear of hitting way past the cup, because the hill helps to slow the ball down. So be firm! Like the best golfers in the world, you will be totally disgusted after leaving an eight-foot uphill putt short.

> **. . . ninety percent of all putts that come up short of the hole never go in.**

STRATEGY:
CHIPPING AND PITCHING

You can lob the ball in high, and have it stop quickly on the green—a **pitch**—or take it in low and roll it across the green up to the cup—a **chip**. **(Figure 80, below)** Think of these two shots in terms of the time spent in the air compared to their time rolling on the ground:

❖ A pitch spends most of its time in the air. At least half of the shot, and maybe as much as four-fifths or more, is off the ground with very little roll once it lands.

❖ A chip spends roughly one-third of the total distance in the air, with two-thirds spent on the green, rolling like a putt.

Keep in mind that trajectory is all-important: a higher shot (the pitch) comes down at a steeper angle with little forward roll once it hits the ground. A lower shot (the chip) has much more forward momentum, causing it to roll after it lands. This section deals with changing the trajectory of your shots   to influence that amount of roll.

Figure 80:

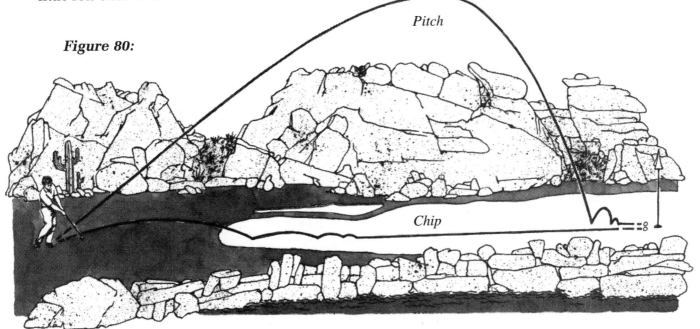

Pitch

Chip

DO I CHIP, OR DO I PITCH?

The first consideration is the putting green: it has the most uniform surface on the golf course. Most often you'll want to land the ball on this smooth surface while avoiding the irregular grass just off the green.

But often you'll be able to take the ball over the rough and land it safely on the green by *either* pitching or chipping. **(Figure 81)** Which one should you use? *Chipping is the percentage shot. Chip when the first third of the shot puts the ball safely on the green.*

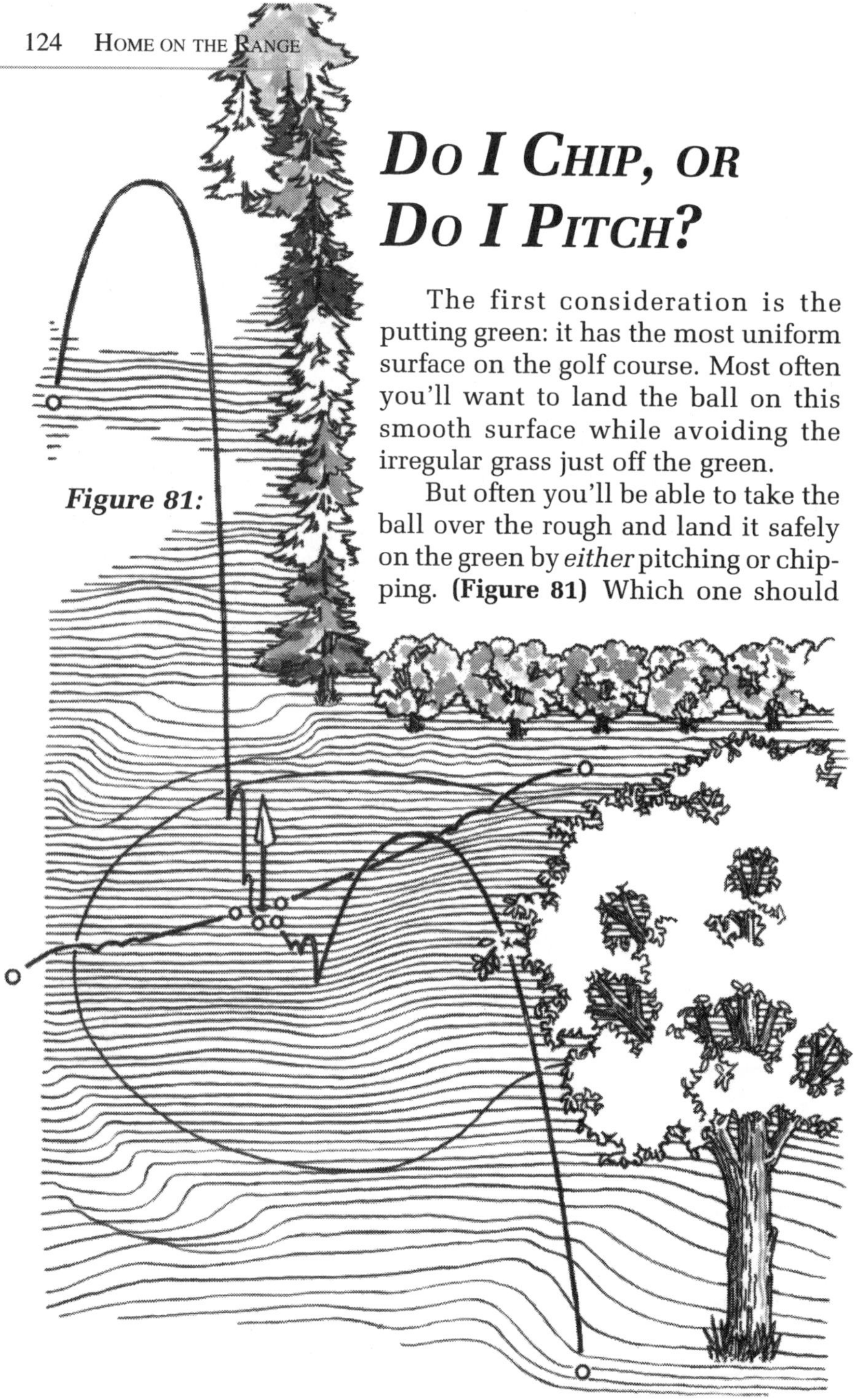

Get into the habit of standing off to the side of the green to look at your short shots. From this vantage point you can accurately judge the distance between your ball and the edge of the green, and the edge of the green to the hole. If you are able to safely carry the area between your ball and the green using the one-third carry, two-thirds roll formula, you should chip. (Landing the ball a minimum of two to five feet onto a relatively flat spot on the green would be a safe margin for error.)

On the other hand, pitch when you have to carry the ball at least half the distance to the hole to land it safely on the green. For example, pin placements that give you very little green to work with, or lobbing over a high-lipped sand bunker with the flag just on the other side, are predicaments that call for a pitch. **(Figure 82)**

Pitches are much more difficult shots to hit than chips. The following three reasons explain the challenge:

1. Pitching takes a longer stroke—more things can go wrong. As you will see, chipping is a simple stroke; with fewer moving parts, it's more repeatable.

2. The landing area is farther away and more difficult to hit when pitching. A closer landing spot helps eye-hand coordination. When chipping,

Figure 81:

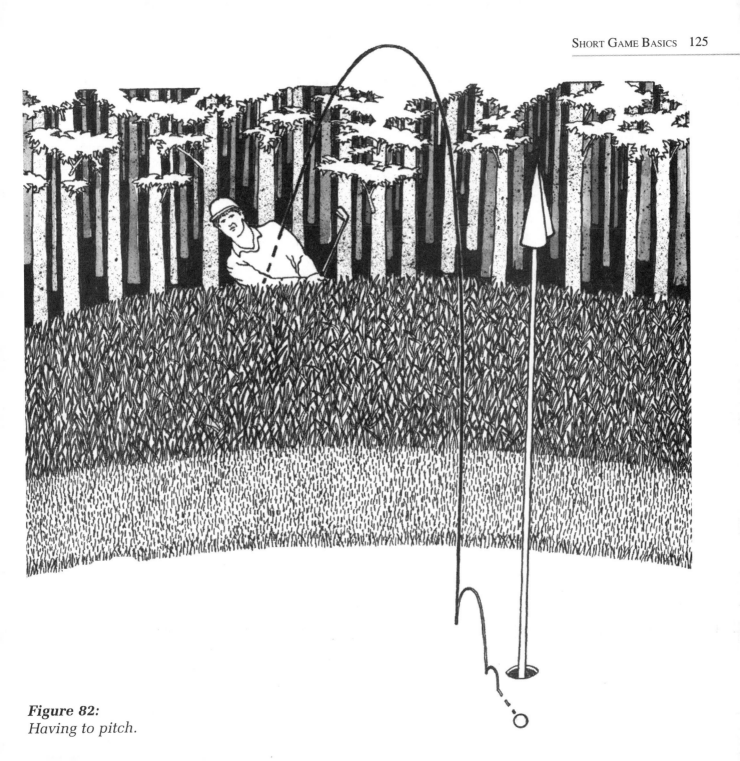

Figure 82:
Having to pitch.

the landing spot on the green is nearer to you than the pitch's; you will accurately hit the chip's landing spot many more times as a result. Imagine tossing pennies to both landing spots underhanded, without a club, and you'll get the idea.

3. The higher your ball gets above the ground, the more the wind blows it around. Notice that, even in a slight breeze, the tops of the trees move a lot more than the lower branches. Because pitching puts the ball up into the wind, you have to compensate, depending on the wind's direction. Chipping, by definition, keeps the ball down out of most of the wind's effects.

DISTANCE CONTROL

See the Landing Spot

For both chipping and pitching, the use of an intermediate target on the green can dramatically improve your results.

Stand to the side and visualize the shot you are about to hit. **(See Figure 80.)** Focus on the first target—*the landing spot*—to get the ball closer to the ultimate target, the hole. Make that spot on the green the last thing you look at before you swing; aim there, not at the hole! Picking the correct landing spot for the type of shot you need is easier when you have a clear picture in your mind of the trajectory and how much roll there will be to the hole after the ball hits the green.

For another way to fine-tune your distance control see **Touch**, next.

Touch

Suppose the next time you work on your short game, the manager of the range comes out and offers $100 (okay, let's be realistic—a free bucket of balls) to the person who can toss a ball underhanded without a club, closest to the hole. Picture the finesse you would use to manufacture this kind of throw (shaped like a chip or pitch), and you'll understand more about the touch needed for the short game.

During this underhanded toss, your arm would swing in a relaxed, smooth, and unhurried fashion. A short backswing would lead into a longer follow-through. After letting go of the ball, your hand would flow out toward the target, guiding the shot to the hole. Finally, the takeaway and the forward swing would be at about the same tempo, without any abrupt acceleration. Keep these images in mind when chipping, pitching, and putting, and your short game (and scores) will improve.

CHIPPING

*The chip is a low, rolling, easy-to-perfect shot, and it's the kind that when mis-hit,
can still put the ball close to the cup. Spend some time on this one—
it will lower your scores immediately.*

SETUP

To create a low rolling shot—a chip—modify your address position in four key ways:

1. Use a less lofted club. Most chips call for an 8-, 7-, 6-, or 5-iron, although there may be times when you choose to use other clubs. *(Some professionals use the sand wedge for all shots around the green, even chips. While a high degree of confidence in a single club may be fostered, I believe this technique takes more talent and time spent practicing than most of us have.)*

2. Instead of playing the ball off the inside of the left heel like in the full swing, move the ball back. Play the ball somewhere between the center of your stance and your *right* heel. This change in ball position decreases the *effective loft* of the club, producing lower shots. (See next paragraph, below.) It also encourages a descending blow for cleaner contact with the ball.

   The position of the ball in your stance greatly effects the trajectory of your shots. Playing the ball back toward your right heel decreases the club's effective loft—the loft of the clubface at impact. Your hands should be just inside your left thigh when striking the ball correctly. With your hands in this position, playing the ball back nearer your right heel causes the shaft of the club to lean more toward the target at impact, with less loft on the clubface and lower shots resulting. **(Figure 83)** On the other side of the coin, a ball played forward in your stance decreases the lean of the shaft at impact, which increases the effective loft. The shot travels higher. **(Figure 84)**

3. Change your weight distribution at address: put sixty percent of your weight on your left foot and keep it there for the entire stroke. Setting your head to the left, in front of the ball, will help. The correct weight distribution leans the grip-end of the shaft toward the target to decrease the clubhead's effective loft at impact. And, like the new ball position, it promotes a descending blow for more solid shots.

4. Finally, keep your hands in their normal full swing location, just opposite the inside of your left thigh. Combined with ball placement and weight distribution, this hand position causes the shaft of the club to lean to the left at address.

Figure 83:
Ball back—
less loft.

Figure 84:
Ball forward—
more loft.

And this alignment from address through impact almost guarantees a low, rolling shot—a chip.

The rest of the address position is similar to the full swing, but now stand nearer to the ball with your eyes closer to the target line; the ends of your toes should not be more than a foot from the target line. You might be uncomfortable at first, but this brings you closer to your work, improving eye-hand coordination. **(Figure 85)** With your feet closer together, point your right foot to 12 o'clock and your left to about 11 o'clock. Tilt your spine forward, with your relaxed arms hanging straight down. Flex your knees, and keep them and your spine set at a constant angle throughout the swing.

Start with your hands lower on the grip, even going as far down as the end of the grip where the metal begins. Choking down allows you to stand closer to the ball, again improving eye-hand coordination and it shortens the club, producing shorter, more controlled shots.

Form a straight line from your left shoulder, left arm and club shaft, down to the clubhead. Your hands should be in their usual full swing position (just off the inside of the left thigh), with the shaft leaning toward the target. See # 4 above.

GRIP

Like the putting stroke, chipping involves a pendulum-type motion of the triangle formed by your arms and shoulders. This stroke is so similar to putting that many pros use their reverse overlap putting grip when chipping. **(See Putting, Grip, page 113.)** They want to keep their wrist action to a minimum in both strokes, which the reverse-overlapping grip is designed to do. With quiet wrists, they can concentrate on moving the triangle formed by their arms and shoulders. When putting (as in many other skills), consistency comes not only with fewer moving parts, but also by putting the big muscles in charge.

Experiment using your normal full swing grip and the reverse-overlapping putting grip, and pick the one that generates the best results.

THE STROKE

Try for a short backswing and a longer follow-through, for the same reasons as in putting: the compact backswing helps you avoid deceleration, and the extended follow-through guides the ball to the cup. Your body should remain reasonably motionless; however, unlike putting,

allow your weight to shift *slightly* toward the target on the downswing, especially on longer chips where it would be awkward to keep your lower body perfectly still. In other words, let your legs support the movement of your upper body.

ONE OTHER THING

Consider making your chipping and putting strokes as similar as possible. They both get the ball rolling on the green, and involve the same execution—weight left, the shaft leaning toward the target, lack of wrists while the triangle moves like a pendulum, etc. Look at it this way: every time you practice your putting, your chipping improves, and vice versa. If you agree, and many touring pros do, then this would be a good time to go back and review **Putting, page 113**.

Figure 85: Standing close to the ball.

PITCHING

One of the best things you can do for your game is to practice pitching. Full shots improve because you are practicing a miniature version of the full swing, and your scores drop due to increased confidence with one of the most difficult shots in golf.

Use this shot to hit the ball high and land softly, with little roll. **(See page 124, Do I Chip or Do I Pitch?)** A pitch, like the full shot, spends most of its time in the air. It has all the other elements of the full swing, too—grip, address, weight shift, follow-through, relaxed upper body, balance, connection, and swing path and plane—only in miniature.

ADDRESS

To get the ball up and landing quietly:
1. Pull out your sand wedge, pitching wedge, or 9-iron, depending on how high the shot needs to be and how soon it must stop on the green. A lofted club produces a more elevated shot that doesn't roll much. A sand wedge gives you the highest, stop-on-a-dime shot of any club in your bag (unless you have a specialty club, like an "L" wedge). The pitching wedge goes a little lower, rolling more after it lands; a 9-iron flies lower and rolls even more.

2. Play the ball somewhere from the middle of your stance to your left heel, like your full swing. This

produces a higher shot because of the increase in effective loft. Put your feet in their usual full swing position, at 11 o'clock for the left and 12 o'clock with the right, but closer together. Choke down a little on the grip to stand closer to the ball, improving eye-hand coordination.

3. Address the ball with your weight evenly distributed between your feet. For a little lower shot, but a chance for cleaner contact with the ball, put slightly more weight on your left foot—about 55 or 60 percent.

BACKSWING

Note that the size of the backswing controls the distance of the pitch; lesser distances require a shorter backswing, and vice versa. We use only a fraction of our normal backswing when pitching—and that helps to make this one of the most difficult shots in golf. Pitches are pure touch shots. We have no backstop for the top of our swing. For example, with a 40-yard pitch shot it's very difficult to tell where the club should stop in the backswing—should it go two-thirds or three-fourths of the way back? That little difference in the size of the backswing can account for as much as 40 yards—20 yards too little, or too much—of the ultimate distance of the shot. Only practice and experience help determine the correct length for the backswing on any given pitch.

DOWNSWING

Stay relaxed and avoid a rushed or hurried swing. Use your legs and hips: not for power as in the full swing, but to create the proper sequence—the lower body leading the upper body through the downswing. Your legs should gently tug your arms down through impact and into the follow-through. *Don't* pull your arms down from the top. Or try to scoop the ball up into the air. Review the full swing chapter on **Leg Drive, page 36**, and apply a compact version of the same principles to the pitch shot.

FOLLOW-THROUGH

There are two basic ways to look at the follow-through in pitching: (1) Tom Kite sees the end of his swing as a mirror image of his backswing. With a three-quarter backswing, he wants a three-quarter follow-through **(Figure**

86); or, (2) Let your arms coast to a natural stop. A longer backswing produces a longer follow-through, and vice versa, but there is no attempt to either restrict or amplify the follow-through. The arms stop naturally, the same way they would when you're pitching pennies, or a ball, under-handed to different distances.

Figure 86:
Backswing mirrored by follow-through.

BUNKER SHOTS

Some people fear hitting out of bunkers more than any other shot in the game. But this can be one of the easier shots you encounter during a round of golf—expert golfers often hope a poor approach shot ends up in the bunker, rather than having to face a tricky lie in the tall grass around the green.

To understand this shot, imagine standing in the bunker holding a big scoop of sand in your open palms, with the ball sitting on top. Throw it all up and away from you, like an explosion, toward the hole—with the ball riding on top of the sand out of the bunker. When hitting an *explosion shot* out of a greenside bunker, the clubhead should not touch the ball, and that accounts for some of the ease in playing this shot. Because your club enters the sand between one and four inches behind the ball, there is a wide margin for error. Hit anywhere in that one-to-four- inch area, and you can get the ball to ride out.

One key to this shot is using the right club. Beginning golfers often overlook the value of carrying a sand wedge in their bag. The sand wedge is unique because it has a high degree of *bounce*. In the early 1930's, Gene Sarazen, one of the greatest golfers ever, modified one of his short irons by adding solder to the bottom of it. He had increased the bounce—and the sand wedge was born.

To see this bounce, hold any of the irons other than a sand wedge out in front of you. Point the shaft straight up and lift the club up until the bottom edge of the clubhead is at eye level. The leading edge (the one that gets to the ball first) is lower than the back edge on all of your irons except the sand wedge, which has the back edge lower than the front. **(Figure 87, next page)** This lowered back edge is the bounce, and it allows the clubhead to slide through the sand, exploding the ball out of the trap without the club digging in.

If you don't carry a sand wedge in your bag, you're limiting yourself to the same equipment and techniques golfers were stuck with before Sarazen's invention more than sixty years ago. It's high time you bought one.

Here's another consideration: because it's called a *sand* wedge doesn't mean you use it only in the sand. This is a terrific scoring club: touring professionals include this club (along with the driver and the putter) on their three-most-used-clubs-during-an-average-round-of-golf list. Remember, the pros aren't in the sand that much. They're using this club often from the grass around the greens.

The extra loft of the sand wedge is essential for many pitch shots from the fairway or rough. It has more loft and weight than any other club (except the 'lob' wedge), so it manufactures the highest, quickest-stopping shots. You'll need it when you are fifty yards from the hole with a tree between your ball and the flag, and have very little green to

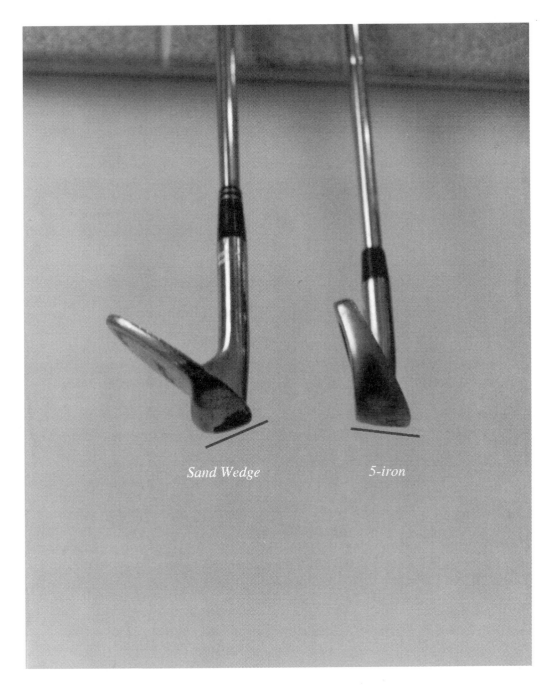

Sand Wedge   5-iron

Figure 87:
The sand wedge's high degree of bounce.

work with. Or if you find yourself in the fairway twenty yards from the flag, with a high-lipped sand trap between your ball and the hole. Instead of using your sand wedge to extricate the ball from the bunker on your next shot, use it to avoid the trap in the first place.

Also, this club is helpful when the ball sits down in deep grass. The added weight of the flange helps carry the club through the grass to get the ball up and out.

Used from the sand, the fairway, or the rough, the sand wedge is the quintessential utility club.

THE SAND SHOTS

Greenside Explosion

1. Walking into the bunker, try to judge the consistency of the sand with your feet. The rules of golf do not allow testing the sand with your hands or club, so other than looking at it, this is the best way to judge its texture. Slowly wiggle your feet back and forth as you address the ball, assessing not only how deep the top layer is, but also whether it's fluffy, firm, or hard-packed. Digging your feet in also improves your balance during the shot, and lowers your body, making it easier to hit one to four inches behind the ball.

2. Set up to the ball with your clubface open (pointing to the right of the target line), and play the ball near the middle of your stance. Opening the clubface increases the effect of the bounce, allowing the club to glide through the sand without digging in. You can open the club to varying degrees to adjust for the specifics of the shot—the condition of the sand, how high the lip of the bunker is, and the distance to the hole. All things being equal, open the clubface more for soft sand, high-lipped bunkers, or when there is very little green between the trap and the hole—in other words, when you need an extra-high shot that stops quickly. On the other hand, when the sand is hard-packed, the bunkers are low-lipped and there is plenty of green between you and the pin, the clubface should be less open or even square to the target line at address.

Because you are aiming one to four inches behind the ball, hold the club over the spot where you want it to enter the sand, not directly behind the ball. Don't touch the sand—grounding your club in any hazard results in a two stroke penalty.

3. Aim your feet and body left of the target line to compensate for the clubface pointing to the right. Try Tom Watson's method—he aims his

SHORT GAME BASICS 135

clubface thirty degrees to the right of the hole, aligns his body thirty degrees to the left, and expects the ball to pop out straight. Another method is to aim your body thirty degrees to the left, but start with the clubface square to the target at address. This way you swing out to the left, but the ball goes where the clubface points at address. Experiment to find the right combination for you.

4. Take a smaller version of your full swing, depending on the distance to be covered. Make sure to swing out to the left of the hole, in the same direction your feet point. If you subconsciously swing toward the hole with a clubface that is open thirty degrees, the ball will end up thirty degrees to the right of the target.

5. Follow through! Otherwise, the ball stays in the bunker without enough clubhead speed to carry the sand out. This is not to say you want to abruptly accelerate down into the ball. Keep the backswing and downswing smooth and evenly paced—but don't quit on it at impact.

Fairway Bunkers

So far I've been discussing greenside sand traps. But when your ball is in a fairway bunker, the shot calls for a different technique, and most likely a change in club selection.

First, consider how high the lip of the bunker is, then look at the distance to the green. The number one priority is to get the ball out of the trap, so choose a club with enough loft to clear the lip even if it means coming up short of the green. Suppose you are 150 yards away and normally from the fairway a 5-iron would cover the distance. From your position standing in the bunker, you see the 5-iron possibly catching the lip of the trap and rolling back down to your feet. You might need to use a more lofted club like an 8-iron to get up over the lip and out of the hazard, even though the shot will come up thirty yards short of the green. It's much better to be out of the bunker on your first attempt than to try a club with too little loft, leave the ball in the trap, and have to hit the same shot all over again.

Square the clubface to the target line at address and dig your golf shoes down into the sand for balance; position the ball farther back in your stance (to the right) than you would for an explosion shot; and put sixty percent of your weight on your left foot. These adjustments encourage clean contact at impact, with the club hitting the ball first. Unlike greenside bunkers, you must strike the ball cleanly; don't contact *any* sand until after impact. Try to take a shallow divot in the sand to the left of the ball.

(See No Power, Divots, page 97; and Divots, page 56.) Pinch the ball and you'll be successful.

Swing normally, but with a quieter lower body for better stability. Stay relaxed and balanced throughout. Because the sand cuts down on your ability to swing fully and still stay in balance, it is a good idea to use more club (less loft) than you need—as long as you can still clear the lip of the bunker. If you are an 8-iron distance away, consider hitting a 7-, or even a 6-iron with an extra-smooth swing. Use your legs to support, rather than drive, your upper body.

There can be a great temptation to look up as you strike the ball, making a topped shot likely—the kind that embeds into the front lip of the trap. To counter this tendency: swing slowly and in balance, keep your spine steady, and don't look up until well after impact.

CHAPTER FIVE

SHORT GAME PROBLEMS AND SOLUTIONS

Look up your specific problem, find the appropriate subheading, and try the bulleted cures until you find the correct fix.

PUTTING

PUTTS: TOO FAR

THE STROKE

The distance a putt travels is determined mostly by the size of the backswing. A good case can be made for keeping it short: (1) a backswing that is too long sends the putt past the hole; (2) combining a short backswing with a longer follow-through helps eliminate deceleration through impact, a prime cause of wayward putts; (3) the shorter the backswing, the less that can go wrong during the stroke—an economy of motion.

These drills should improve your touch by limiting your backswing enough to get the ball into the cup, or into an imaginary circle around it.

❖ Simply work on a shorter backswing. Without aiming at anything, choose a flat portion of the green and take your address position. Put a tee in the ground to serve as a backstop, six inches behind the ball. Don't take the putter any farther back than this tee. Keep your stroke smooth and make sure your follow-through is longer than your backswing to avoid deceleration. Mentally record the distance produced.

❖   Put the putter away and use your hand instead. Pick a target and roll the ball underhanded, trying to leave the ball as close to the hole as possible. Notice the length of your backswing on the ones that get close. Your hand goes back only far enough to propel the ball that distance to the cup, with no hint of deceleration through impact. Rehearse that same size stroke with your putter to get a feel for the distance. **(See Touch, page 126.)**

❖   You won't be going for the hole with this drill. Pick an empty spot on the practice green, well away from other people. Set up a row of six tees parallel to, and just outside, your target line. Space the tees two inches apart and play the ball opposite the tee on the left. **(Figure 88)** Hit five balls, taking the putter back to the farthest tee (to the right of the ball). Then hit five balls taking the putter back to the second farthest tee, gradually working your way to the tees closer to the ball. If your stroke is smooth, with the same tempo back and through, each group of five balls should cluster in roughly the same spot, at distances corresponding to the size of your backswing. For the best results, put the ball on the same spot on the green each time and don't decelerate. Your touch on the greens should improve when the relationship between the length of the backswing and the distance the ball travels becomes ingrained.

Figure 88:
The Tee Drill

❖   Choose a hole on a level part of the green so you won't have to compensate for an uphill, downhill or breaking putt—your concern here is touch. Drop four balls on the target line, three feet from the cup. After making all four putts from three feet, move back to try six-footers. If you only sink two putts, stay at this distance. But if you sink three or more, move back to nine feet. Continue this pattern, increasing the putts by three feet each time—on an extension of the same target line of the first three-foot putts. If you don't make at least two putts, go back to the *beginning*—the three-footers, and work your way back up to the longer distances. When hitting the progressively longer putts, the only change in your stroke should be the length of your backswing, not the tempo or effort of your swing. And remember to use a pendulum stroke, with the same evenly paced swing away from, and through, the ball—your main concern should be to accurately gauge the distance. This drill instills confidence from close range because you'll often have to go back to hitting those three-footers, and it has a positive effect on the longer ones because they are just an extension of the same straight-in shorter putts.

❖ Here's a drill from Tom Watson: To improve your sense of the distance required, try putting with your eyes closed. Alternate between stroking a ball normally and putting from the same spot with your eyes closed. Concentrate on your feel. You'll be getting it when your second (sightless) putt comes to rest next to the first. Your feel for distance will improve as you learn to resist the urge to look up. This drill also helps you trust your stroke—if you can putt well with your eyes closed, think how much more confidence you'll have with them open.

Many golfers take a smooth backswing, then abruptly accelerate and wail at the ball coming back down. Instead of stroking *through* the ball, they end up hitting *at* it. Keep everything evenly paced and smooth using a pendulum-type stroke, with the same speed coming through as going back.

❖ Try to imagine, as Jack Nicklaus does, that the shaft of the putter is a hollow glass tube with very thin walls. Don't let it shatter during impact with the ball.

❖ Imagine the putter head is made of solid rubber with the ball rebounding off it softly, not with a lot of noise and fanfare.

LOSING FEEL
Getting tied up in the mechanics of the stroke can cause a loss of feel. You won't hit the ball the correct distance when thinking more about technique than making the putt. **(See Touch, page 126.)**

❖ Spend a part of your practice time ignoring technique. Using some of the drills above, focus only on getting the putt to roll the correct distance.

READING THE GREEN
You must take into account the downhill slopes on the green. Rehearse reading your putts, even (especially) on the practice green.

❖ **Review Reading the Greens, page 119.**

PUTTS: TOO SHORT

THE STROKE
Backswings that are too big lead to deceleration. Subconsciously, we know if we come down the same way we went back, we'll hit the ball to the other end of the green. Through impact, we ease into the ball to try to salvage our touch—and the ball comes up short.

❖ Put your putter back in the bag and use your hand instead. Roll the ball underhand, and try to leave it as near to the hole as possible. Notice how short your backswing is on the close ones. Your hand goes back only far enough to propel the ball the exact distance to the cup, and with no hint of deceleration through impact. Rehearse that same stroke with your putter to get a feel for the distance. **(See Touch, page 126.)**

❖ Work on a shorter backswing—only enough to get the ball into the cup or a circle around it. **(See Putting Strategies, A Bigger Target, page 121.)** Now you can accelerate through impact.

❖ On the other hand—though it's unusual—your backswing could be too short. Remember, the distance needed to get the ball to the hole is governed by the length of the backswing. **(See Putts: Too Far, page 137.)** Take the putter head back far enough to get the ball to the cup.

READING THE GREEN
Take into account the uphill slope of the green. Practice reading your putts, even on the practice green at the driving range.
❖ **Review Reading the Greens, page 119.**

MISSING THE SWEET SPOT
Without solid contact between the putter and ball, the shot comes up short.
❖ The first step is to figure out exactly where your putter's sweet spot is. Mark it and hit the ball there every time. **(See Finding the Sweet Spot, next page.)**

❖ To strike the ball there at impact, make sure the sweet spot of your putter is directly behind the ball at address.

❖ Turn the triangle formed by your shoulders, arms, and hands in one piece back and through the stroke. Disconnecting your arms from your shoulders when putting has the same effect as during your full swing—inconsistent shots, partly due to the inability to hit the ball on the sweet spot. Flipping your wrists around during the stroke (aggravated by disconnection) contributes to this same problem. The bottom line is that the bigger muscles, e.g., your shoulders, should be in charge of *all* your swings. They tend to move the same consistent way time after time. **(See The Stroke, page 118.)**

❖ Keep your head and spine as still as possible throughout the stroke, especially through impact. Don't peek! The littlest movement makes it very difficult to get back to impact in the same position you started from, causing you to miss the sweet spot.

❖ EXPERIMENT: You can buy a kind of tape made to attach to the front of your clubface to indicate the location of impact. It shows up as a darker area against the white background. Check with your local golf shop for this tape.

Finding the Sweet Spot

Hold the grip of the putter between your left index finger and thumb. Pointing the toe toward you, lift the club up so that the head of the putter hangs at about waist level. With a golf ball held in your right hand, start tapping the right side of the putter head near the toe, and gradually tap back toward the middle and then toward the heel. Notice how the club wobbles when struck in the toe and heel area. Somewhere in the middle is the most balanced part of the putter face—the sweet spot—an area where the club doesn't wobble or twist in your hand. If that spot is marked on the club, double check it with the method above to determine its accuracy. If it's not accurate, or if there is no mark, put your own dot on the club. Use a metal file or a dab of paint to mark the correct spot on the *top* of the putter—so you can see it as you look down at address. For a more thorough and detailed method of finding your particular putter's sweet spot, see the excellent Dave Pelz book, *Putt Like the Pros.*

PUTTS: LEFT AND RIGHT

GRIP
A strong or weak grip can cause the clubface to open or shut at impact, sending your putts astray.
❖ Consider using a neutral grip when putting—where the back of the left hand and the palm of the right face the target. Since both hands should be square with the clubface, think of striking and guiding the ball to the hole with the palm of your right hand or the back of your left. Another option is to turn both hands out, with the palms in an opposing alignment. **(See Figure 72B, page 115.)** This can help keep wrist action to a minimum, allowing you to repeatedly square the clubhead at impact.

ADDRESS
Striking the ball with the wrong part of the putter causes many off-line putts.
❖ Put the sweet spot of the putter directly behind the ball at address; try to contact the ball with that part of the club at impact. **(See Finding the Sweet Spot, previous page.)**

AIMING AND ALIGNMENT
To hit the ball straight, the putter needs to travel along the target line at impact. Faulty alignment changes your swing path, leading to pushes to the right and pulls to the left.
❖ Check that the *bottom* leading edge of the putter is perpendicular to the target line.

❖ Set your toes, knees, hips, and particularly your shoulders parallel to the target line. After taking your address, have a friend lay an extra club across your shoulders: it should parallel the target line. It's important to check your forearms in the same manner. **(See Figure 76, page 117.)**

❖ Think carefully about these imaginary lines across your toes, knees, hips, and shoulders. For right handers, these lines should be parallel *left* of the target line—aimed slightly to the left of the target. **(See Figure 16B, page 28.)** If the lines of your body point directly at the target, a line parallel to your body and through the ball will aim to the right. Your ball will start to the right of the target even with the perfect stroke.

❖ Use the putter as an alignment aid. After finishing the stroke, and without moving your feet, lay the shaft of your putter on the green across your toes. Now move behind the club to look down the line to the target. The line of the club and the target line should be parallel to each other and *not* converge off in the distance.

❖ Poor alignment can also occur if your eyes are too far from the target line and ball. Put your eyes directly above the target line or slightly inside the line. After taking your address, hold the club at the very end of the grip and let it hang straight down from the bridge of your nose. Look down the shaft at the ground; if the club hangs directly over the ball, or just inside the line, then so do your eyes. **(Figure 89)**

Figure 89:
Checking position
of eyes at address.

❖ Most often the line your putt must travel on won't be straight from the ball to the cup because of the slope of the green. To compensate for this break, don't aim at the hole—aim in the direction you want the ball to start before it curves back to the hole. The outermost point of the expected curve of the putt is the spot to aim and swing toward. **(See figures 78 and 79, page 120.)**

SWING PATH

❖ After aligning your shoulders correctly at address, put them in control of the stroke. **(See Wrists below, and review Connection, page 54.)**

❖ Try to guide the clubhead out to the target on the follow-through with your left hand. Or feel as though you are pushing it toward the target with your right hand. But don't use either hand independently of your shoulders.

WRISTS

Turning or scooping your wrists through impact directly effects the clubface.

❖ Concentrate on moving just the triangle formed by your shoulders and arms. Put your shoulders in charge of the stroke and keep the independent movement of your hands to a minimum. **(Review Connection, page 54.)**

EXCESSIVE MOVEMENT OF HEAD AND SPINE

❖ Keep your body, especially your head, still during the stroke; don't look up until you hear the ball go in the cup. Move the triangle only.

MISSING THE SWEET SPOT

Hitting the ball off the heel of the putter causes misses to the left of the cup, while hitting off the toe makes it go right: the impact with the ball causes the clubface to twist (almost imperceptibly), sending the ball wherever the putter ends up pointing.

❖ The first step is to figure out exactly where your putter's sweet spot is. Mark it and try to strike the ball there every time. **(See Finding the Sweet Spot, page 141.)**

❖ To hit the ball there at impact, put the sweet spot of your putter directly behind the ball at address.

❖ Turn the triangle formed by your shoulders, arms, and hands in one piece back and through the stroke. Disconnecting your arms from your shoulders when putting has the same effect as during your full swing—inconsistent shots, partly due to the inability to hit the ball on the sweet spot. Flipping your wrists around during the stroke (aggravated by disconnection) does the same. The bottom line is that the bigger parts of your body, e.g., your shoulders, should be in charge of all your swings. They tend to move the same consistent way time after time. **(See Putting, The Stroke, page 118.)**

❖ Keep your head and spine as still as possible throughout the stroke, especially through impact. Don't peek! The littlest movement makes it very difficult to get back to impact in the same position you started from, causing you to miss the sweet spot.

❖ EXPERIMENT: You can buy a kind of tape made to attach to the front of your clubface to indicate the location of impact. It shows up as a darker area against the white background. Check with your local golf shop for this tape.

EQUIPMENT
Make sure the rubber (or leather) grip was installed correctly, especially if you put it on yourself.
❖ Most putter grips are flat along the top edge where the thumbs usually rest. Look down the shaft from the grip end to see if this flat edge is perpendicular to the bottom leading edge of your putter. If not, have the grip reinstalled.

CHIPPING

Many good golfers make putting and chipping as similar as possible, so by practicing one they improve the other. That means the problems for each can also be very similar—check first to see if your chipping problem is listed under Putting, Problems and Solutions, starting on page 137.

CHIPS: TOPPING

STROKE

Swinging the clubhead too high above the ground is the most common reason for topping a chip. Properly done, the club makes contact with the grass to the left of the ball, and it touches the ground, not just the tops of the blades of grass. The inability to brush the grass as deeply as that means the clubhead is too high, with the leading edge contacting the ball close to its equator.

❖ Take plenty of practice swings without the ball. Learn to brush the grass down by the roots. Don't cut your follow-through short just because you are concentrating on making contact with the grass. Keep it smooth!

BALL POSITION

With your ball too far forward in your stance, the club moves upward at impact. The bottom edge of the club can easily hit the top of the ball.

❖ Position the ball somewhere between the middle of your stance and your right heel to play a low, running shot—a chip. Take some practice swings without the ball to see where your club is contacting the grass. Play the ball a quarter-inch to the right of that spot. **(See Chipping, Setup, #2, page 127.)**

WEIGHT DISTRIBUTION

Sixty percent of your weight should be on your left foot at address and through impact. Incorrectly leaning back on your right foot causes the club to move up at impact, topping the ball. **(See Chipping, Setup, #3, page 127.)**

❖ Position your head in front of the ball and keep it there; this puts most of your weight on your left foot, allowing you to hit down and pinch the ball.

CHANGING YOUR LEVELS

Keep your head, spine, and knees at the same level throughout your swing. Lifting your body takes the club along, too.

❖ Watch the ball until well after impact. See the spot where the ball used to be before looking up to see where it went.

❖ Lightly touch your forehead against an imaginary wall at address and through impact. **(See Figure 51, page 70.)**

❖ Imagine a metal pole running down your back and into the ground, keeping your spine in position at address and during the swing. As your shoulders turn, your spine should stay against this pole—until well after impact. **(See Figure 51, page 70.)**

❖ Keep your knees flexed to the same degree throughout the stroke.

CHIPS: TOO FAR

TRYING THE WRONG SHOT

It's possible you shouldn't be chipping. If you try to hit a low shot onto the putting surface when you should be pitching, you can easily misjudge the distance; for example, chipping without enough green to work with can cause the ball to roll well past the hole. **(See page 124, Do I Chip, or Do I Pitch?)**

❖ After choosing a spot to hit from, survey the shot from the side to judge the correct carry and roll. **(See Figure 80, page 123.)** Walk the length of your shot, calculating both the overall distance to the hole and the span between your ball and the edge of the green. If you can land the ball safely on the green one-third of the distance to the hole, chip. If you have to carry the ball halfway (or more) to safely avoid the fringe, pitch.

BALL POSITION

The closer the ball is played to your right heel, the less effective loft the clubface has at impact. This causes the shot to come off the clubface at a lower angle, resulting in more roll.

❖ Move the ball forward slightly (but no farther than the middle of your stance) until you find the right combination of about one-third carry and two-thirds roll.

WEIGHT DISTRIBUTION

With too much (more than sixty percent) of your weight on your left foot at address, you'll be decreasing the *effective loft* at impact and increasing the roll of the ball.

❖ Distribute sixty percent of your weight on your left foot, forty percent on your right.

❖ Double-check your hand position, making sure your hands are opposite the inside of your left thigh. Don't let your hands drift forward to the outside (to the left) of your left thigh—this can cause you to lean your whole body too far to the left, not to mention delofting the clubface.

WRONG CLUB

When using a club with too little loft, the ball travels lower, lands with more forward momentum, and rolls past the cup.

❖ Experiment with the different clubs in your bag to find the right combination of carry and roll from various distances and in different conditions. Wind, wet greens, and difficult lies greatly affect club selection. An 8-, 7-, or 6-iron work well for most chips.

BACKSWING

The size of your backswing governs the length of the chip.

❖ Limit the size of your backswing. Find some reference points to help you judge how far to take the club back to hit the ball certain distances. For example, focus on taking the clubhead back no farther than just past your right foot. That might give you a 15-foot chip with an 8-iron; taking the clubhead back to knee-high could create a 25- or 30-foot chip. Or focus on your hands—swinging your hands back to the middle of your right thigh could produce a 10-foot shot, while taking your hands to hip-high might be good for 35 feet.

❖ Get into the habit of taking a couple of practice swings to rehearse the size of your backswing.

HITTING AT THE BALL

A sudden acceleration of the clubhead at the ball on the downswing can cause your chips to race past the hole. Gain more consistency from your chips by keeping the same smooth tempo coming down as when taking the club back. Remember, your chipping and putting strokes should have a similar pendulum motion, hitting *through* the ball, not *at* it.

❖ Mimic the pendulum of a grandfather clock when moving the triangle formed by your arms and shoulders, and take the club back and through the ball smoothly.

❖ Throw ten balls underhand without a club, shaping the shot like a chip. Try to get the ball to roll up even with the cup. Think of swinging with that same easy touch when the club is in your hands. **(See Touch, page 126.)**

❖ Imagine that the shaft of your club is made of a hollow tube of thin glass. Don't break the shaft at impact.

❖ Often we lean on the club, pushing it down into the ground at address. Our tempo is wrecked immediately with the club catching in the grass on the way back. Instead, try holding the club slightly above the ground at address. This contributes to a smoother and more connected swing.

MISJUDGING THE LANDING SPOT

Aiming for the hole instead of where the ball should land on the green is a common mistake. When the ball carries to the hole and *then* takes its roll, say good-bye to par. Remember, the real target is the landing spot on the green: concentrate on landing the ball there.

❖ The first step is to figure out where to land the ball. Without a club, throw ten balls underhand, trying to shape them like chip shots. Mentally record where the ball landed on the best tosses—the ones that had a low trajectory and finished right up next to the cup. That's your landing spot.

❖ Physically mark the landing spot with a tee, a ball, a leaf, or anything handy. Land your ball as near to that spot as possible.

❖ Make sure the landing spot is the last thing you look at before swinging, *not* the hole.

Corey Waggoner

Because of an excessive use of his hands, Corey faced inconsistent distance with his chips. Now, having quieted his hands and wrists, he encounters many more one-putt greens.

Time Spent on Project:
5 Weeks

Average Score: 95

Practice Schedule:
3 times per Week

Playing Schedule:
2 times per Week

Lowest Score: 78

Playing Since: 1993

Occupation:
Clothing Import/Export

WRISTS

The hinging and unhinging of your wrists produces clubhead speed. If they hinge and unhinge when chipping, your wrists can send the ball too far. **(Figure 90, below)** The following cures help firm your wrists during this stroke:

❖ The line from your left shoulder and down the club should be as straight at the finish as it was at address. **(Figure 91, below)**

❖ At the end of your swing, the grip end of the club should point to the same place on your shirt that it did at address. If it points past the right side of your body, your wrists have moved during the swing.

❖ When gripping down on the shaft, keep the upper part of the grip against your left forearm *throughout* the stroke. Imagine a rubber band securing the club against your forearm. **(Figure 91, insert, below)**

❖ Think of your hands going past the ball before the clubhead reaches it.

❖ Use the reverse-overlap putting grip to decrease wrist action.

Figure 90

Figure 91

CHIPS: TOO SHORT

BALL POSITION

Playing the ball too far forward in your stance increases the effective loft of the club, causing the shot to go higher and come down at a steeper angle, with less roll. **(See Chipping, Setup, #2, page 127.)**

❖ Gradually move the ball back in your stance, half an inch at a time, until you get the one-third carry, two-thirds roll shape to your shot. The correct ball position will be somewhere between the middle of your stance and your right heel.

WEIGHT DISTRIBUTION

With too much weight on your right foot, your head will be behind the ball at impact. This tilt of your body increases the effective loft of the club, creating higher shots with less roll.

❖ Putting your head to the left of the ball at address, position the ball off your right cheek. This helps get sixty percent of your weight on your left foot.

❖ Set your hands opposite the inside of your left thigh at address, which tends to automatically put more weight to the left.

WRONG CLUB

When using a club with too much loft (a 9-iron or pitching wedge, for example), the ball goes higher and drops from the sky at a steeper angle without much roll after it lands.

❖ Experiment with the different clubs in your bag to find the right combination of carry and roll from various distances and in different conditions. An 8-, 7-, or 6-iron work well for most chips.

DECELERATION

The ball is likely to come up short when the club slows down through impact. Two problems create deceleration:

Taking the club back too far. With a huge backswing for a short shot, instinctively you'll realize that you are about to send the ball over the green. To compensate, you may try to ease into the ball while trying to keep the shot under control.

❖ Limit your backswing. It is surprising how short your backswing can be to still get the ball to the hole. Use reference points to help judge various distances. **(See Chipping, Too Far, Backswing, page 148.)** Remember to follow through out to the hole; feel as if you are guiding or pushing the ball there.

❖ Always take at least one practice swing to rehearse the size and pace of the shot. Get into this habit at the range so it carries over to the course.

Taking the club back too quickly. With a rushed backswing, you will sense you're about to hit a bigger shot than necessary. A decelerating downswing will be a last ditch attempt at controlling the shot.

❖ Move the triangle formed by your shoulders and arms in one piece. Put your shoulders in charge of the backswing (instead of your arms and hands) and turn this triangle with your shoulders. Your shoulders move more slowly because they are a bigger part of your body. **(See Putting, The Stroke, page 118.)**

❖ Throw ten balls underhand without a club, trying to shape them like chip shots. Etch this tempo in your mind and use it when hitting the ball with the club. **(See Touch, page 126.)**

❖ Take slower-motion practice swings.

MISJUDGING THE LANDING SPOT
The landing spot needs to be out far enough on the target line for the ball to make it to the hole.

❖ Mark a landing spot on the practice green about one third of the way to the hole with a tee, a ball, or some other object. Land your ball as close to that spot as possible.

❖ Throw ten balls underhand, trying to shape them like chip shots. When a ball (with the correct trajectory) stops next to the cup, note where it first hit the green—that's your landing spot. **(See Touch, page 126.)**

❖ Always have a spot in mind and make landing the ball *there* the last thing you think about before taking your backswing.

WRISTS (SCOOPING)
Flipping your wrists at the ball leans the shaft of the club back away from the target, increasing the effective loft at impact. The ball goes too high and lands without enough forward roll.

❖ The line from your left shoulder and down the club should be as straight at the finish as it was at address. **(See Figure 91, page 150.)**

❖ At the end of your swing, the grip end of the club should point to the same place on your shirt that it did at address. If it points past the right side of your body, your wrists have moved during the swing.

❖ When gripping down on the shaft, keep the upper part of the grip against your left forearm *throughout* the stroke. Imagine a rubber band securing the club against your forearm. **(See Figure 91's insert, page 150.)**

❖ Think of your hands going past the ball before the clubhead reaches it.

❖ Use the reverse-overlap putting grip to decrease wrist action.

TOPPING
On long chips, especially when hitting the ball over deep or wet grass, a thin shot can get caught up and probably won't make it to the green.
❖ **See Chips: Topping, page 146.**

CHIPS: *LEFT AND RIGHT*

GRIP
A strong or weak grip can cause the clubface to open or shut at impact, sending your chips off line.
❖ Consider using a neutral grip when chipping—where the back of the left hand and the palm of the right face the target. Since both hands should be square with the clubface, think of striking and guiding the ball to the hole with the palm of your right hand or the back of your left. Another option is to turn both hands out, with the palms in an opposing alignment. **(See Figure 72B, page 115.)** This can help keep wrist action to a minimum, allowing you to repeatedly square the clubhead at impact.

ALIGNMENT
To hit the ball straight, your club needs to travel along the target line at impact. Faulty alignment changes the swing path and leads to pushes to the right and pulls to the left.

❖ Check that the bottom leading edge of your club is perpendicular to the target line.

❖ Set your toes, knees, hips, and particularly your shoulders parallel to the target line. After taking your address, have a friend lay an extra club across your shoulders: it should parallel the target line. It's important to check your forearms in the same manner. **(See Figure 76, page 117.)**

❖ Think carefully about these imaginary lines across your toes, knees, hips, and shoulders. For right handers, these lines should be parallel *left* of the target line—aimed slightly to the left of the target. **(See Figure 16B, page 28.)** If the lines of your body point directly at the target, a line parallel to your body and through the ball will aim to the right. Your ball will start to the right of the target even with the perfect stroke.

❖ Use your club as an alignment aid. After finishing the stroke, and without moving your feet, lay the shaft of the club on the ground across your toes. Now move behind the club to look down the line to the target. The line of the club and the target line should be parallel to each other and *not* converge off in the distance.

❖ Poor alignment can also occur if your eyes are too far from the target line and ball. Hang your eyes slightly inside the line. After taking your address, hold the club at the very end of the grip and let it hang straight down from the bridge of your nose. Look down the shaft at the ground; if the club hangs just inside the line, then so do your eyes. **(See Figure 89, page 143.)**

❖ Often the line your chip must travel on won't be straight from the ball to the cup because of the slope of the green. To compensate for this break, don't aim at the hole—aim in the direction you want the ball to start before it curves back to the hole. **(See Figures 78 and 79, page 120.)**

PATH
Turning or scooping your wrists through impact directly effects the path of the clubface.

❖ Concentrate on moving just the triangle formed by your shoulders and arms. Put your shoulders in charge of the stroke and keep the independent movement of your hands to a minimum. **(Review Full Swing Basics, Connection, page 54.)**

EXCESSIVE MOVEMENT OF HEAD AND SPINE
❖ Keep your upper body, especially your head, still during the stroke. Move the triangle only. **(Review The Spine, page 33.)**

CHIPS: *SHANKS AND OFF THE TOE*

Ultimately, both shanks and toed shots come from missing the sweet spot.
❖ Concentrate on moving just the triangle formed by your shoulders and arms. Put your shoulders in charge of the stroke and keep the independent movement of your hands to a minimum. **(Review Full Swing Basics, Connection, page 54.)**

❖ To hit the ball there at impact, put the sweet spot of your club directly behind the ball at address.

EXCESSIVE MOVEMENT OF HEAD AND SPINE
❖ Keep your head and spine as still as possible throughout the stroke, especially through impact. Don't peek! The littlest movement makes it very difficult to get back to impact in the same position you started from, causing you to miss the sweet spot.

WRISTS
The following cures help firm your wrists during this stroke:
❖ The line from your left shoulder and down the club should be as straight at the finish as it was at address. **(See Figure 91, page 150.)**

❖ At the end of your swing, the grip end of the club should point to the same place on your shirt that it did at address. If it points past the right side of your body, your wrists have moved during the swing.

❖ When gripping down on the shaft, keep the upper part of the grip against your left forearm *throughout* the stroke. Imagine a rubber band securing the club against your forearm. **(See Figure 91's insert, page 150.)**

❖ Think of your hands going past the ball before the clubhead reaches it.

❖ The reverse-overlap putting grip decreases wrist action. **(Pages 113-115)**

PITCHING

Because pitching is basically a miniature full swing, the first place to look for a cure is in the Full Swing Problems and Solutions section starting on page 61. Then check here for cures unique to pitching.

PITCHES: *THIN SHOTS*

When pitch shots go bad, topping is the most common result. All the same causes of thin full shots apply here, so be sure and check the Full Swing Problems and Solutions section for help. But the following are two other problem areas to consider:

WRISTS (SCOOPING)
Your wrists are a hinge; once the clubhead passes your wrists, it has to move up. Flipping your wrists through impact causes the bottom edge of the clubhead to contact the ball on its way up.

❖   Try to get your hands to pass the ball before the clubhead reaches it. Feel as though the clubhead is lagging behind your hands through impact.

❖   Ala Nick Faldo, keep the back of your right hand as close as you can to your right forearm, on the downswing and through impact. **(See Figure 66, page 100)**

REVERSE WEIGHT SHIFT
Your neck is also a hinge; after the clubhead passes your neck, it has to move up. If you finish with most of your weight on your right foot, it's likely your head has moved to the right on the downswing, causing the bottom edge of the club to move upward at impact, striking the top of the ball.

❖   Finish in the correct position: a miniature follow-through, with your right heel off the ground, just the inside edge of your right big toe touching the ground, and less than ten percent of your weight on your right foot.

❖   Standing in the follow-through, look for a straight line up your left leg, shoulders, head and spine.

PITCHES: *FAT SHOTS*

CHILI-DIPPING

Have you ever found yourself in this position? Twenty yards off the green with your pitching wedge in hand, you've lined up perfectly to hit a nice little shot that stops just short of the pin. On the downswing, disaster strikes. The turf flies, but your ball doesn't. It feels like you didn't even touch the ball—because you didn't. You have just "chili-dipped," an apt description popularized by Lee Trevino. Your club slowed down as it approached the ball, causing it to take out the ground behind the ball and leaving you without a follow-through. *Deceleration* is the primary cause of chili-dipping. Two problems create deceleration:

Taking the club back too far. With a huge backswing for a short shot, instinctively you'll realize that you are about to send the ball over the green. To compensate, you may ease into the ball while trying to keep the shot under control.

❖ Limit your backswing. It is surprising how short your backswing can be to still get the ball to the hole. Use reference points to help judge various distances. **(See Chips: Too Far, Backswing, page 148.)** Remember to follow through out to the hole; feel as if you are guiding or pushing the ball to the hole.

❖ Always take at least one practice swing to rehearse the size and pace of the shot. Get into this habit at the range so it carries over out on the course.

Taking the club back too quickly. With a rushed backswing, you will sense you're about to hit a bigger shot than necessary. A decelerating downswing will be a last ditch attempt at controlling the shot.

❖ Move the triangle formed by your shoulders and arms in one piece. Put your shoulders in charge of the backswing (instead of your arms and hands) and turn this triangle with your shoulders. Your shoulders move more slowly because they are a bigger part of your body. **(See The Stroke, page 118.)**

❖ Throw ten balls underhand without a club, trying to shape them like pitches. Etch this tempo in your mind and use it when hitting the ball with the club. **(See Touch, page 126.)**

❖ Take slower-motion practice swings.

PITCHES: TOO FAR

BALL POSITION

The closer the ball is played to your right heel, the less effective loft the clubface has at impact. This causes the shot to come off the clubface at a lower angle, resulting in more roll and too much distance. **(See Chipping, Setup, #2, page 127.)**

❖ Move the ball slightly forward (but no farther than your left heel) until you see one-half or more carry in the air and little roll.

WEIGHT DISTRIBUTION

With too much (more than sixty percent) of your weight on your left foot at address, you'll be decreasing the effective loft at impact and increasing the roll of the ball.

❖ Put no more than fifty five percent of your weight on your left foot at address (fifty percent may be best).

❖ Double-check your hand position, making sure your hands are opposite the *inside* of your left thigh. Don't let your hands drift forward to the outside (to the left) of your left thigh—this can cause you to lean your whole body (along with the club shaft) to the left, completely delofting the club.

WRONG CLUB

When using a club with too little loft, the ball travels lower, lands with more forward momentum, and rolls past the cup.

❖ Experiment with the different clubs in your bag to find the right combination of carry and roll from various distances and in different conditions. Keep in mind that wet greens, wind, and difficult lies greatly affect club selection. A sand wedge or pitching wedge work best for most standard pitches.

BACKSWING

The size of your backswing governs the length of the pitch.

❖ Limit the size of your backswing. Find some reference points to help you judge how far to take the club back to hit the ball certain distances. For example, focus on taking the *clubhead* back to about hip-high. That might give you a 25-yard shot with a sand wedge; taking the clubhead back shoulder-high could create a 40- or 50-yard pitch. Or focus on your *hands*—swinging your hands back to the middle of your right thigh could produce a 15-yard shot, while taking your hands to hip-high might be good for 25 yards.

❖ Get into the habit of taking a couple of practice swings to rehearse the size of your backswing.

HITTING AT THE BALL

A sudden acceleration of the clubhead at the ball on the downswing can cause your shots to fly past the hole. Gain more consistency by keeping the same smooth tempo coming down as when taking the club back. Remember, hit *through* the ball, not *at* it.

❖ Think of the pendulum of a grandfather clock when moving the triangle formed by your arms and shoulders, and take the club back and through the ball smoothly.

❖ Throw ten balls underhand without a club, shaping the shot like a pitch. Try to get the ball to roll up even with the cup. Think of swinging with that same easy touch when the club is in your hands. **(See Touch, page 126.)**

❖ Often we lean on the club, pushing it down into the ground at address. Our tempo is wrecked immediately with the club catching in the grass on the way back. Instead, try holding the club slightly above the ground at address. This contributes to a smoother and more connected swing.

MISJUDGING THE LANDING SPOT

Aiming for the hole instead of where the ball should land on the green is a common mistake. When the ball carries to the hole and *then* takes its roll, say good-bye to par. Remember, the real target is the landing spot on the green: concentrate on landing the ball there.

❖ The first step is to figure out where to land the ball. Without a club, throw ten balls underhand, trying to shape them like pitch shots. Mentally record where the ball landed on the best tosses—the ones that had a high trajectory, little roll, and finished right up next to the cup. That's your landing spot.

❖ Physically mark the landing spot with a tee, a ball, a leaf, or anything handy. Land your ball as near to that spot as possible.

❖ Make sure the landing spot is the last thing you look at before swinging, *not* the hole.

PITCHES: *TOO SHORT*

DECELERATION

The ball is likely to come up short when the club slows down through impact. Two problems create deceleration:

Taking the club back too far. With a huge backswing for a short shot, instinctively you'll realize that you are about to send the ball over the green. To compensate, you may ease into the ball while trying to keep the shot under control.

❖ Limit your backswing. It is surprising how short your backswing can be to still get the ball to the hole. Use reference points to help judge various distances. **(See Chips, Too Far, Backswing, page 148.)** Remember to follow through out to the hole; feel as if you are guiding or pushing the ball in that direction.

❖ Always take at least one practice swing to rehearse the size and pace of the shot. Get into this habit at the range so it carries over out on the course.

Taking the club back too quickly. With a rushed backswing, you'll sense you're about to hit a bigger shot than necessary. A decelerating downswing will be a last ditch attempt at controlling the shot.

❖ Move the triangle formed by your shoulders and arms in one piece. Put your shoulders in charge of the backswing (instead of your arms and hands) and turn this triangle with your shoulders. Your shoulders move more slowly because they are a bigger part of your body. **(Putting, The Stroke, page 118.)**

❖ Throw ten balls underhand without a club, trying to shape them like pitch shots. Etch this tempo in your mind and use it when hitting the ball with the club. **(See Touch, page 126.)**

❖ Take slower-motion practice swings.

MISJUDGING THE LANDING SPOT

The landing spot needs to be out far enough on the target line for the ball to make it to the hole.

❖ Mark a landing spot on the practice green, one-half to four-fifths of the way to the hole, with a tee, a ball, or some other object. Land your ball as close to that spot as possible.

❖ Throw ten balls underhand, trying to shape them like pitches. When a ball (with the correct trajectory) stops next to the cup, note where it first hit the green: that's your landing spot. **(See Touch, page 126.)**

❖ Always have a spot in mind and make landing the ball *there* the last thing you think about before taking your backswing.

BUNKER SHOTS

Sand shots resemble pitches and are also very similar to the full swing. Look for many of the cures to your sand problems in Full Swing (and Pitching) Problems and Solutions. Then check this section for cures unique to sand shots.

THE SAND: *LEAVING IT IN BUNKER*

GRIP
It is imperative that the face of your sand wedge stay open, pointing to the right of the target line, through impact. This activates the bounce of the sand wedge, popping the ball out of the trap. A strong grip (turned to the right) has the opposite effect, shutting down the club and causing it to dig in. The clubhead goes too deeply into the sand, leaving the ball in the bunker.
❖   Take a weak grip, with both palms turned slightly to the left at address. **(See Figure 12, page 24.)** This keeps the face open through impact (pointing to the right), activating the bounce of the sand wedge.

GRIP PRESSURE
❖   A light grip pressure encourages a fluid, unhurried swing. The club is more likely to follow through without decelerating. Imagine holding an uncapped tube of toothpaste, a room temperature stick of butter, or a live bird. Don't squeeze any of them, from the beginning to the end of your swing. **(See Grip Pressure, page 21.)**

SWING
Make sure your backswing is long enough to get the ball out of the bunker. A short, quick swing can compress the sand as the clubhead contacts it. The resistance of this compacted sand slows down the club enough that the ball won't get out.
❖   Try to swing as slowly, and fluidly, as possible. Exaggerate this feeling while practicing at the range.

LUNGING DOWN AT THE BALL

Because bunker shots are uncomfortable for most amateur golfers, the tendency is to try to get the shot over with as soon as possible. Jerking the club down can lower your body, causing you to hit too deeply into the sand.

❖ **Review Fat Shots, Excess Movement of the Spine and Head, page 83; and Casting, page 85.**

DECELERATION

You must finish your swing to get out of the sand consistently. Two problems create deceleration:

Taking the club back too far. With a huge backswing for a short shot, instinctively you'll realize that you are about to send the ball over the green. To compensate, you may ease into the ball while trying to keep the shot under control.

❖ Limit your backswing. It's surprising how short your backswing can be to still get the ball to the hole. Use reference points to help judge various distances. **(See Chipping, Too Far, Backswing, page 148.)** Remember to follow through out to the hole; feel as if you are guiding or pushing the ball there.

❖ Always take at least one practice swing to rehearse the size and pace of the shot. When playing on the course, you'll get penalty strokes for touching the sand while taking a practice swing; take this swing well above the sand, or stand outside the bunker while practicing.

Taking the club back too quickly. With a rushed backswing, you will sense you're about to hit a bigger shot than necessary. A decelerating downswing will be a last ditch attempt at controlling the shot.

❖ Move the triangle formed by your shoulders and arms in one piece. Put your shoulders in charge of the backswing (instead of your arms and hands) and turn this triangle with your shoulders. Your shoulders move slowly because they are a bigger part of your body. **(See Putting, The Stroke, page 118.)**

❖ Think of your arms moving at the same speed away from, and down toward the ball.

❖ Take slow-motion practice swings.

THE SAND: SKULLING THE BALL

Topped shots in a bunker can leave the ball in the sand, or send the ball flying across the green.

❖ **See Full Swing Problems and Solutions, Thin Shots, page 75.**

❖ Concentrate on hitting the sand one to four inches behind the ball. Try to get the clubhead to enter the sand there. Don't look at the ball, or you might hit *it* instead of the sand.

THE SAND: INCORRECT DISTANCE

MISJUDGING THE LANDING SPOT

❖ Make the landing spot the last thing you look at before swinging, *not* the hole. **(See Pitches: Too Far, Misjudging the Landing Spot, page 159.)**

THE SAND: INCORRECT DIRECTION

ADDRESS

Because greenside explosion shots call for an open clubface at address, take extra care with the alignment of your toes, knees, hips, and shoulders. Pointing the clubface to the right at address while aligning your body *square* to the target line causes the ball to miss to the right of the target.

❖ Aim your body—toes, knees, hips, and especially shoulders—to the *left* of the target to compensate for the open clubface. **(See Greenside Explosion Shots, #2 and #3, page 134.)**

BUYING CLUBS

Buying properly fitted clubs is one of the first steps to becoming a good golfer. Because we are all built differently, our clubs need to be fitted to us as individuals.

A wise purchase for any level golfer—from beginner to low handicapper—is a set of clubs built to one's specifications, including: shaft length, lie angle, face angle, grip size, grip style, club head design, swing weight, shaft flex, flexpoint, and shaft composition.

I've seen students delay buying good quality clubs until becoming a better golfer—a golfer deserving of better equipment. They didn't want to waste their money on clubs they might end up discarding because of lack of ability.

But because they initially purchased inexpensive ill-fitting clubs, their progress was held back. Many people have actually quit playing golf because no matter how conscientiously they practiced, their poorly made clubs kept them from improving.

In my view, if you know you like the sport and are going to play it for a while, buy the best-fitting equipment you can lay your hands on. Here are some of the necessaries:

Grip size

A grip too big in circumference for your hands won't allow your wrists to unhinge correctly through impact, holding the clubface open and forcing the ball to the right. The opposite can occur if the grip is too small.

Lie

Formed at the bottom of the hosel, this is the angle between the shaft of the club and clubhead. This angle effects the way the clubface sits on the ground at address and has everything to do with where the ball goes. A properly fitted club will rest with 2/3rds of the bottom edge (the 2/3rds closest to the heel of the club) on the ground, and the remaining 1/3rd (out by the toe) slightly in the air. The club actually points to the right at impact if the toe touches the ground at address—the lie angle would be too flat. On the other hand, the club is aimed too far left if the toe and most of the bottom edge of the club is off the ground—

the lie is too upright. Using a special machine, this lie angle needs to be adjusted so that every iron in your set fits you.

Loft

The angle the clubface leans back, relative to the shaft, can be adjusted to maximize the trajectory of your shots. For example, those of you living in the breezy Southwest could consider having some loft taken off your clubs to help keep the ball under the effects of the wind.

For most, leaving the lofts at standard is a good idea, with the possible exceptions of the wedges (pitching and sand) and long irons.

Shaft length

When giving your children a set of clubs, be careful! Changing the length of a club influences many factors, including the shaft flex, lie angle, and swing weight. When cutting down adult-sized clubs to fit a youngster, for example, keep in mind: shortening a shaft stiffens it, sometimes to the point of making it unplayable. On the other hand it also flattens the lie, which generally will be helpful to a shorter person. All of this illustrates the need for an expertly run fitting session— whether purchasing for kids or adults.

Shaft flex

The forces in the golf swing cause the club's shaft to bend, greatly effecting where, and how far, the ball travels. Theoretically, a softer shaft will kick forward more at impact, increasing distance. But along with longer shots could come a degree of wildness from all that flexing. Conversely, a stiffer shaft could supply you with more control, but shorter shots. (I say "theoretically" because most better players I know have all experienced longer shots after switching to stiff shafts. All the more reason to test drive different shaft flexes to see what you experience.)

Shaft flexpoint

Exactly where does the club shaft bend? If that point is close to the ball, a higher shot will result. If the club bends more toward the grip-end, the ball will go lower.

Shaft material

The two basic choices are steel and graphite. Graphite feels terrific but is more expensive. Because of it's shock-absorbing properties, graphite can be a great choice for people with joint problems, for example, arthritis in the hands and/or wrists.

Club head design

Forged or cast? Or another way to put it is, do you want to play with a blade or cavity-back designed iron? Becoming popular in the 1970's, cavity-back clubs have just that—a cavity carved out of the back of the clubhead. Most people would agree that this design creates a bigger area on the clubface in which to hit a solid shot. On the other hand, some would argue that feel and the ability to work the ball (curve it one way or the other on purpose) are lost.

Swing weight

This measures how heavy the grip-end of the club is compared to the head-end. While you don't want the end of the club to feel like a bowling ball when you swing it, you also don't want the sensation of swinging a tooth pick or pencil, either.

While the golf professional at your local range will be able to give you expert advice about the proper grip size and lie angle for you, make sure you demo different clubs. Try various shaft flexes, different shaft materials, and clubhead designs to find the ones most appealing to you.

GLOSSARY

Address: The position in which a golfer stands to the ball.

Blading the ball: Hitting too high up on the ball with the bottom leading edge of the clubface.

Blocking: Incorrectly positioned arms through impact causing shots off the toe, thin shots, and slices.

Bounce: The protruding back edge at the bottom of sand wedges.

Break: The slope of a putting green.

Bunker: A hazard, normally made of sand, but they can also be filled with grass.

Casting: The premature unhinging of the wrists on the downswing, causing hooks, loss of clubhead speed, fat and thin shots, and a distorted swing plane/path.

Chili-dip: A totally flubbed pitch or chip, mostly due to deceleration. These shots are hit fat with the ball advancing not more than a few feet.

Chip: A low, rolling shot played from closer to the green.

Closed stance: Addressing the ball with the right foot pulled back away from the target line.

Coming over the top: The right shoulder, arm, and hands moving out toward the target line immediately on the downswing, causing the clubhead to move on an outside-to-in path.

Divot: The section of ground removed during the golf swing.

Draw: A shot that starts straight, then curves gently from right to left.

Driver: The 1-wood.

Effective loft: The loft of the clubface at impact.

Fade: A shot that starts straight, then curves gently from left to right.

Fairway woods: Used from the fairway or tee, they are more lofted and shorter than the driver and include the 7-, 5-, 4-, and 3-woods.

Fat shot: Hitting the ground before the ball is struck.

Hosel: The part of the clubhead the shaft connects to.

Hook: A shot that starts straight, then curves out-of-control from right to left.

Late hit: The wrists unhinging (correctly) later in the swing, down near impact.

Lie: The angle formed between the bottom edge of the clubface and the shaft entering the hosel.

Loft: The degree to which the clubface leans back, pointing skyward.

Neutral grip: Holding the club with both the back of the left hand and the palm of the right pointing toward the target.

Open stance: Addressing the ball with the left foot pulled back away from the target line.

Pitch: A high shot with little roll, played from closer to the green.

Pull: A shot that starts immediately to the left, and continues on in that same direction.

Pull hook: A shot that starts immediately to the left, before curving farther left.

Pull slice: A shot that starts immediately to the left, before curving back to the right.

Putt: A stroke made using a putter with the ball remaining on the ground, rolling.

Push: A shot that starts immediately to the right, and continues straight in the same direction.

Push slice: A shot that starts immediately to the right, before curving farther right.

Reading the greens: Determining the eventual curve of a putt, due to the slope of a green.

Releasing: Correctly positioned arms through impact; promotes clubhead speed and a square clubface at impact.

Reverse weight shift: Shifting weight in the wrong direction, toward the target, during the backswing.

Rhythm: The speed of the backswing as it relates to the speed of the downswing.

Shanks: Hitting the ball with the club's hosel, instead of the sweet spot.

Short game: Shots played from on, or near, the green with a partial swing; these include: putting, chipping, pitching, and greenside bunker shots.

Skulling the ball: Hitting too high on the ball with the bottom leading edge of the clubface.

Slice: A shot that starts straight, then curves out-of-control from left to right.

Square stance: Addressing the ball with both feet, knees, hips, and shoulders the same distance from the target line.

Strong grip: Holding the club with both the back of the left hand and the palm of the right pointing up and to the right of the target.

Sweet spot: The most balanced part of the clubface.

Target line: The imaginary line stretching from the ball to the target.

Tee shot: Played from within the tee box and normally with the ball sitting on a wooden tee. This is the first shot on any given hole.

Tempo: The overall speed of the swing.

Thin shots: Hitting too high on the ball with the bottom leading edge of the clubface.

Topping the ball: Hitting too high on the ball with the bottom leading edge of the clubface.

Waggle: A slight movement of the club at address, used in most pre-shot routines to relax the golfer's hands and forearms, and as a rehearsal for the takeaway.

Weak grip: Holding the club with both the back of the left hand and the palm of the right pointing left of the target and down toward the ground.

Whiff: Taking a swing at the ball but missing it completely.

SPECIAL REPORTS

BY DOUG MCDONALD

Although the following subjects don't belong in a book about the driving range, they do belong on the reading list of every serious golfer. To order, see the form on page 186.

Special Report 1

Course Management and Strategy

Avoid those mental errors that cost valuable strokes in every round. Finally learn to handle on-course conditions—side-hill lies, wind, the pressure of making each shot count, your anger. Use specific strategies like your own *personal par* to play conservatively when you must, and boldly when the opportunity presents itself. Includes many stroke-saving ideas for the golf course.

Practical Considerations

This section covers some of the most important and basic considerations dealing with life on the golf course, including: the significance of the different colored tee markers and flags, figuring out course yardage, and understanding everything on the scorecard. Also your clubs: how are they different from each other and how far should you be hitting them, and what to do if they're all going the same distance.

Rules, Etiquette

Do you know when to use the rules in your favor? Or how to avoid being banned from your friend's game because of poor conduct on the course? This report will help ease you into the flow of the game, painlessly and without embarrassment.

Buying Golf Equipment

Buying equipment can be intimidating. Take golf balls for example: do you need Surlyn or Balata, 90 or 100 compression, 2- or 3-piece, and what about all those dimples? Now get all the information you need to make an educated buying decision about balls, woods, irons, bags, gloves, putters, videos, even sunscreen!

Special Report Number 1 (includes all of the above):
ISBN 0-9628642-8-5 $15.95

To order please turn to page 186.

Special Report 2

Working the Ball: High, Low, Fade, Draw

With many holes designed to accept ideally shaped shots, and obstacles preventing direct access to the green for your approach shots, this information gives you a plan and the means to carry it out. This report shows you how to mold your shots—but now you'll be able to do it on purpose, instead of when you least expect it. Learn to keep the ball low under the wind, to get it up over trees, and to curve it around barriers like houses—hey, what are you doing over there by those houses?

Playing in Poor Weather: Wind, Rain, Hot, Cold

Slippery grips and cold hands can spell disaster on the golf course. And in the summer it's imperative you stay cool and focused. This report contains many techniques to lessen the impact of weather conditions—so you can focus on hitting your best shots. Learn to keep dry, warm, and even-tempered enough to beat your friends.

Golf Exercises

Staying in shape helps free us from injury, adds yards to our shots, and improves concentration—especially when walking up those last few holes. Here you'll find safe and proven techniques for working golf-specific muscles.

Special Report Number 2:
ISBN 0-9628642-7-7 $15.95

To order these reports or *Home on the Range*, please turn to page 186.

RECOMMENDED PRODUCTS

Many students, especially those new to golf, are curious about the best equipment, books, shoes, etc. While the final analysis is always subjective, here's what I use and what I recommend to my students. (Keep in mind: those brands not included here are not necessarily poorly conceived or produced. It could be that I have no personal experience with them. The important thing for you is to try as many products as possible to find your preferences.)

Balls
- Titleist—90 compression, Surlyn
- Maxfli—90 compression, Surlyn

Irons
- Redbird

Woods (metal head)
- Redbird
- Callaway
- Taylor Made
- Ping

Putters
- Ping
- Ram—Zebra
- Spalding—TPM
- Acushnet—Bullseye

Video Tapes
- *Golf My Way*—Jack Nicklaus
- Sybervision

Gloves
- Footjoy
- Titleist
- Mizuno

Shoes
- Footjoy
- Nike
- Etonic

Bags (w/stand attached)
- Jones
- Ping
- Sun Mountain

Books
- *USGA Rules of Golf*
- *Exercise Guide to Better Golf*—Jobe, Yocum, Mottram, Pink
- *How to Perfect Your Golf Swing*—Jimmy Ballard
- *Getting Up and Down*—Tom Watson
- *Putt Like the Pro's*—Dave Pelz
- *Golf My Way*—Jack Nicklaus
- *The Inside Path to Better Golf*—Peter Kostis

INDEX

NOTES:

NOTES:

NOTES:

NOTES:

NOTES:

NOTES:

ORDER FORM

Prices: *Home on the Range* **$15.95**; Special Report #1 **$15.95**; Special Report #2 **$15.95**

Telephone Orders:

Call (206) 522-8940 anytime and have your Visa or MasterCard ready. On the recording leave:

- What you're ordering, including quantity
- Your Visa or MasterCard number
- Expiration date

- The full name on the credit card
- Your address, including city, state, and zip code
- Phone number, including area code

Fax Orders:

(206) 937-1493 Please send this completed form <u>without</u> a cover sheet (to reduce paper waste).

Postal Orders: Send to: Golf in the 80's, P.O. Box 16590-1, Seattle, WA 98116, USA

Please send the following books and reports:

QTY. _____   QTY. _____
QTY. _____   QTY. _____

❏ Check (US Funds Only) ❏ Money Order
      ❏ Credit Card: ❏ Visa, ❏ MasterCard
      Card Number _____
      Name on Card _____
      Expiration Date _____

      Signature _____
      Name _____
      Mailing Address _____
      State_____ Zip _____
      Telephone (w/area code) _____

Sales tax: Please add 8.2% for books shipped to Washington State addresses.

Shipping and Handling:

Standard: $3.50 for the first book or report, and $2.50 for each additional publication. (Surface shipping may take three to four weeks.) **2 to 3 Day Rush:** $5.50 for the first book or report, and $3.50 for each additional publication.

These publications make great gifts for any golfer in your life.
Call, fax, or write and order now.